To Laurie, Lisa, Kelly, and Christiana,
our daughters and sisters
and the mothers of
our grandchildren, nieces, and nephews.
—Sam & Andrew

Page 175 constitutes an extension of the copyright page.

Library of Congress Cataloging-in-Publication Data
Wyly, Sam.
Texas got it right! / by Sam and Andrew Wyly; foreword by
Walter Isaacson. — 1st ed.
  p. cm.
Includes index.
ISBN 978-1-59591-074-5 — ISBN 1-59591-074-3
1. Economic development—Texas. 2. Entrepreneurship—
Texas. 3. Texas—Economic policy. 4. Texas—Economic
conditions—21st century. 5. Texas—Social conditions—21st
century. I. Wyly, Andrew. II. Title.
HC107.T4W95 2012
330.9764–dc23
                                    2012027769

First edition, 2012

10 9 8 7 6 5 4 3 2

Printed and bound in the United States of America

Produced by Melcher Media, Inc. for WYLYBOOKS

TEXAS
GOT IT
RIGHT!

SAM WYLY & ANDREW WYLY
FOREWORD BY WALTER ISAACSON

MELCHER
MEDIA

CONTENTS

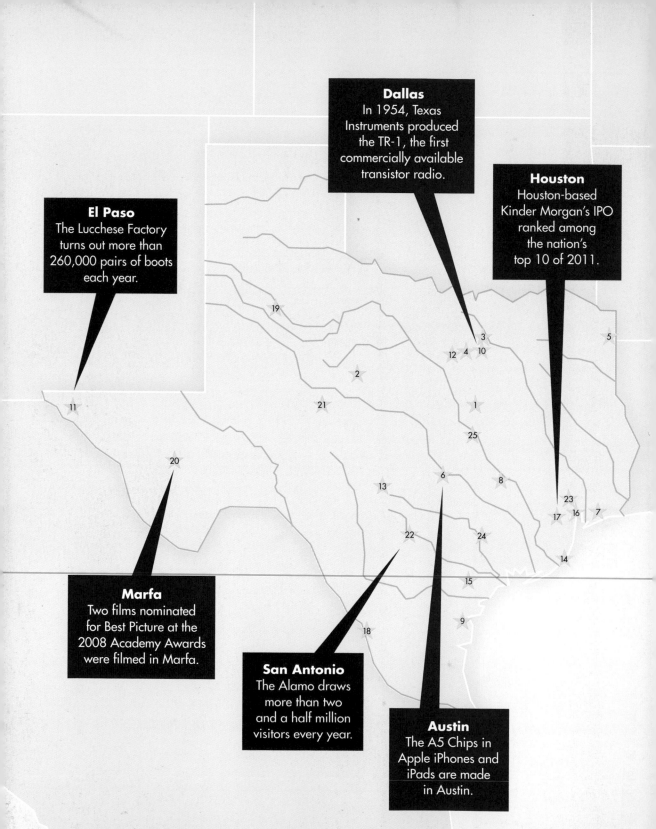

El Paso
The Lucchese Factory turns out more than 260,000 pairs of boots each year.

Dallas
In 1954, Texas Instruments produced the TR-1, the first commercially available transistor radio.

Houston
Houston-based Kinder Morgan's IPO ranked among the nation's top 10 of 2011.

Marfa
Two films nominated for Best Picture at the 2008 Academy Awards were filmed in Marfa.

San Antonio
The Alamo draws more than two and a half million visitors every year.

Austin
The A5 Chips in Apple iPhones and iPads are made in Austin.

19

11

20

2

21

13

22

18

3

12 4 10

5

1

25

6

8

23

17 16 7

24

14

15

9

THE GREAT STATE OF TEXAS

Here's a quick look at just a handful of our favorite Texas places, ones that help define the Texas we know today.

★ *FOREWORD* ★
BY WALTER ISAACSON

Those of us who hail from Louisiana have always been fascinated by the outsize ways of our neighbors in Texas, with their wildcat economic style, ten-gallon-hat personalities, and colorful populist politicians of both parties. So it's particularly exciting for me to have the Texas mystique explained by a native Louisiana guy who became a true Texan, Sam Wyly. His coauthor—son Andrew—is also a true Texan by choice, but one who hails from California, which is a state that serves as a counter-example to the Texas model.

Sam has grown six different companies to billion-dollar valuations, so he realizes that the key to the Texas success story is providing fertile ground for entrepreneurs. We all know that Texas has been an energy pioneer ever since 1937, when the companies that became Chevron and ExxonMobil began drilling offshore. Today that tradition continues with Texas as a pioneer of the shale-oil boom and of wind farming. But Texas was also a birthplace of the microchip. And that tech tradition continues to flower now that Austin has become the hot place for start-ups that connect creative thinking with technology.

In our times, the word *trailblazer* has become such a cliché that we pay little heed to what it means. Texans, however, have bred into their personalities the legacy of the true trailblazers: those cow herders of the Texas plains who blazed new trails and roads in order to get their livestock to markets.

This business and entrepreneurial mind-set also led to a tradition of political leaders who were not just professional partisans but who instead knew how to be dealmakers, in the tradition of Bob Strauss. In California, 80 percent of state legislators consider that role their full-time occupation. For folks in the Texas legislature, that figure is less than 2 percent. They tend, instead, to be farmers, fire-fighters, car dealers, oil-field workers, and business owners. In addition, Texas politicians come in all stripes: progressives, populists, libertarians, right-wing firebrands, and occasional revolutionaries. The one thing most of them have in common is that they are colorful.

The Wylys also celebrate—rather than stoke fears about—the great migrations that have made Texas a "majority-minority" state, one in which Hispanics, blacks, and Asians make up a majority of the population. In praising the largely Hispanic border area, the Wylys write that it "is the most richly Texan of places, because the people who live there know that opportunity resides in what unites us and not what divides us."

Even if you think that not everything about Texas is perfect, and even if you love your own home state more, this book is valuable. Colorful and fun, it is bursting with little facts and big ideas. It all adds up to an important celebration of the spicy mix of ingredients—and the exuberance—that has made Texas successful over the years. The state's can-do spirit and love of independent thinkers, innovators, and entrepreneurs is something that could help kick up our whole economy.

★ PREFACE ★

BY ANDREW WYLY

I went to college at Denison University, a small liberal-arts institution in Ohio with only a few thousand students. One year I invited my schoolmate, a guy from Newark, Ohio, to come with me on a visit to Dallas to see my dad. Driving from the airport, I noticed that my friend kept looking out the car window with a perplexed look on his face. "Where is the desert?" he asked.

"What desert?" I replied.

Like many people visiting Texas for the first time, my friend assumed that the state looked like something out of an old Western movie, a place where men wore ten-gallon hats and boots with spurs, and the landscape was all tumbleweeds and oil wells. But here we were in a teeming, modern city filled with people of every age and race, and bustling with commercial and cultural activity. Given all the mythology surrounding Texas, I guess it's not surprising that outsiders might still harbor some old-fashioned notion about the place and its inhabitants, but the disconnect between fantasy and reality never ceases to amaze me.

I've got an interesting perspective on the Lone Star State. Growing up, I split my time between California and Texas. Shortly after graduating from college in 2004, I decided to leave Los Angeles and move to Dallas. It was a career decision as much as a personal one: Sure, California had a great climate and nice beaches, but the business environment, even in those prerecession years, felt stagnant, burdened with some of the heaviest taxes in the nation and some of the most restrictive regulations. Texas, by contrast, felt vibrant, alive with opportunity.

I also couldn't believe how much cheaper it was to live in Texas. Actually, it was cheaper to do almost anything here, including starting a business, which is what I did in 2007, establishing a film-production company in Dallas in order to pursue my dream of making movies. The fact that I started a career as a film producer *after* leaving Los Angeles says a lot about how much more attractive Texas is than California for young entrepreneurs.

I found that out the hard way when it came time for me to start making my first film. Bowing to conventional wisdom, I decided to shoot most of it back in L.A., figuring that's where so much of the skilled talent in the industry was concentrated. I quickly learned, though, that L.A. is a terrible place to shoot a movie. It is a nightmare of endless paperwork, unscrupulous contractors, and property owners trying to milk extra dollars out of their burdensomely expensive real estate. A common exchange would go like this:

"Hello, I would like to rent your parking lot for a week."

"Sure, it's $100 a day. What do you need it for?"

"I'm making a movie."

"Oh, in that case it's $200 a day."

Months after we finished principal filming, I returned with my crew to Texas to shoot some pickup scenes. I was shocked at how much easier it was.

Above: Andrew Wyly poses for David Wright's painting *The Alamo* in Dripping Springs, Texas. Opposite: The not-in-my-backyarders in other states fight against expanding offshore drilling, but that attitude doesn't fly in Texas.

Obtaining licenses was a comparative breeze, and the costs for everything, from equipment rentals to meals, were much lower. People were just friendlier. A hotel even let us shoot on its rooftop for free.

What is it that makes Texas so special; what makes it such fertile ground for entrepreneurs? An argument could be made that we have a lot of land and that we are mineral-rich. But Alaska is even bigger, geographically, with a wealth of minerals, and it is not growing like Texas. The fact is, a big part of what makes Texas great is not what it has but what it *doesn't have*. Namely, it doesn't have a bloated government bureaucracy with a vast regulatory system that impedes the launching and growth of businesses. Our state constitution limits state legislative sessions to 140 days every other year, making for highly efficient, streamlined lawmaking. And yet the government we do have protects individual rights and private property fiercely. Texans have always taken justice very seriously, and we have some of the toughest penalties for lawbreakers in the country. We also have the Texas Rangers, one of the most illustrious law-enforcement units in the world.

Actually, one of the only apprehensions I did have about moving to Texas was that I'd be miles away from my favorite burger joint, In-n-Out Burger, a California-based, family-owned chain that prides itself on its ultrafresh, high-quality ingredients. For years the company has resisted expanding beyond the reach of its California-based meat-processing facility, meaning that if you wanted an In-n-Out burger, you would have to live in either California or a nearby state such as Nevada, Arizona, or Utah. But in 2010, to my delight, In-n-Out announced that it was restructuring its system and opening a second processing facility just south of Dallas. It's no coincidence that In-n-Out chose the Lone Star State for the company's first-ever expansion outside its home region. It selected Texas for the same reasons that *Chief Executive* magazine has rated our state the number-one place to do business in the country (and California the worst) eight years and running. When it comes to being business-friendly, Texas puts its money where its mouth is.

Restrictions on Offshore Drilling

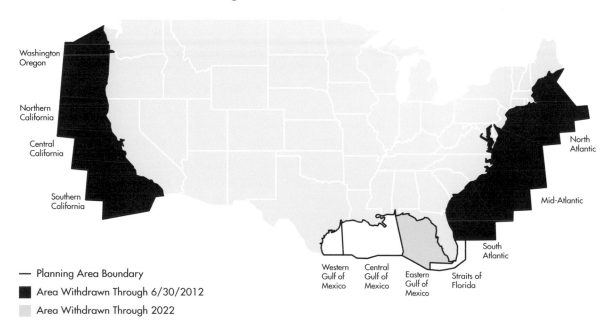

One day I was discussing the theme of this book with a friend from Venezuela. I explained to him that a big chunk of Texas's prosperity owes to two simple things: low taxes and few regulations (the very same factors *Chief Executive* magazine most consistently cites in its rankings). "What about all your oil?" my friend challenged. "Your state must get a lot of wealth from its oil revenues." His assumption reflected an understandable confusion, given where he grew up. Venezuela, like many other countries around the world, has nationalized its oil industry to finance its government, to the enormous detriment of the private oil companies that had developed the infrastructure and technology for extracting all that oil. We Texans wouldn't do anything like that, I explained, because from the beginning we've recognized the primacy of private mineral rights. Texas will prosper only by working together with oil companies and individual property owners to mutual benefit. Judging from Venezuela's present-day economic and social problems, nationalization, if anything, has failed the very people it claimed to benefit.

Indeed, that's something that sets Texans apart: a sense that private energy development goes hand in hand with every other kind of development. I recently attended an environmental conference hosted by the Aspen Institute. At one of the forums a young woman from California received an award for leading a successful effort to shut down a gas-to-liquid processing plant—essential for converting natural gas into clean-burning fuel for combustion engines—that was slated to be built near her home in Santa Monica. *How can this be?* I thought. The City of Santa Monica proudly advertises that its buses run on liquid gas instead of diesel. And yet one of the city's residents was being rewarded for kicking out the very source of that clean fuel—to say nothing of the jobs the plant would have attracted to her town. It was the NIMBY ("Not in My Back Yard") mentality taken to the extreme—a principle some have appropriately called BANANA (Build Absolutely Nothing Anywhere Near Anyone). That kind of knee-jerk response to energy development doesn't go over too well in Texas.

Texans are business-minded, first and foremost, but that doesn't mean we're not progress-minded. As an investor in and an employee of Green Mountain Energy, the Austin-based renewable-power utility, I've learned a lot about striking the balance between the two. Before my time at Green Mountain, I didn't realize how expensive the technology for solar- and wind-energy development is. Turbines used to capture energy from wind and panels used to collect energy from the sun create significantly fewer units of energy for every unit of infrastructure when compared with fossil fuels like oil and coal, which contain a very large concentration of BTUs in a very compact volume. When Texas launched its groundbreaking private electricity market in the early 2000s, Green Mountain saw a chance to make clean energy not just available but *profitable*, by combining natural-gas operations with wind-energy projects to deliver electricity at a price that could compete with that of coal-powered sources.

Back in 2004, a lot of my L.A. friends thought it was strange that I'd want to move to Texas from California. Eight years later, a few of them are probably wishing they'd done the same. Today the California economy is stalling, its population growth is flatlining, and its political clout is waning. Residents of the Golden State are fleeing to Texas in ever-greater numbers, as are Northeasterners and Midwesterners. And once here, they're staying put. In my mind, Texas today is a lot like Paris in the 1920s. Back then, the most innovative and creative writers and artists were breaking the staid confines of Prohibition-era America to taste the freedom of Paris when it was the artistic and literary capital of the world. Today, the best and brightest are flocking to Texas. Like Paris a century or so ago, Texas is having its own golden age. But unlike Paris's, ours is built to last.

★ INTRODUCTION ★
BY SAM WYLY

"Not only is labor not dishonorable among such a people, but it is held in honor; the prejudice is not against it, but in its favor."

—Alexis de Tocqueville,
Democracy in America, Volume 2, 1840

De Tocqueville could easily have been talking about modern-day Texas when he wrote those words about America in 1840. That's because Texans aren't interested in who your daddy was or where you went to school. We don't care what you did in Tennessee or California or New York or Illinois or wherever you came from before you landed in the Lone Star State. If you're ready to work hard, we'll give you the benefit of the doubt. Blood and baccalaureate don't matter to us. We care more about what you *do* than where you're from.

This doesn't mean Texans are blind to the past. After all, we're part of the South, a place where, as Faulkner said, "the past is never dead. It's not even past." We're mindful of our bygone triumphs and defeats. "Remember the Alamo" is just the beginning. We also remember Sam Houston's victory at San Jacinto, where my great-great-uncle, Alfred Wyly, led a company of Tennesseans. And we remember Goliad, where an early Texas Declaration of Independence was

Sam Wyly is the quintessential Texas entrepreneur—a migrant from Louisiana by way of Michigan who has been successfully starting companies and busting up monopolies in Texas since the 1960s.

signed by, among others, another great-great-uncle of mine, Christopher A. Parker, before he became one of the 187 heroes of the Alamo in 1836. We remember the grit of Texas's first settlers—dirt farmers who scratched a living out of the hard earth and laid the foundation for the Lone Star Nation. We remember the great cotton and lumber barons who helped turn our towns into cities, and we remember when that first oil well at Spindletop blew in East Texas in 1901, ushering the age of cars and planes and launching a thousand fortunes. We remember the crash of the 1980s, too, when so many of those Texas oil fortunes went belly-up and new fifty-story skyscrapers in Dallas and Houston remained "see-through" empty buildings for ten years.

Those were tough times for Texans, but we're optimists by nature—probably the most stubbornly optimistic people on earth. We see opportunity where others see disaster. In 1987, when real estate here collapsed after oil dropped from $40 per barrel to $9, I moved my company, Sterling Software, across the street to a half-vacant building rent-free for two years. Our three companies came out of those hard times just fine. Texas did, too.

That's because Texans aren't afraid to fail. And when we do, we don't beg for taxpayer bailouts. Just ask Richard Fisher, the head of the Dallas Fed. He's been preaching against "too big to fail" for years now, a voice of Main Street common sense in a room full of East Coast policy wonks. He looks back on the 1980s S&L crisis in Texas and sees survivors that came out stronger and leaner and ready to grow. Today Texas banks outperform the rest of the nation's banks fivefold, and our pioneers' homestead laws, which protect citizens from predatory creditors, helped Texans avoid the subprime mess. Fisher—who is trying to instill Lone Star fiscal responsibility in

The Spanish, French, and British Empires of North America, 1776. Texas was instrumental in successively pushing the great European empires off the continent.

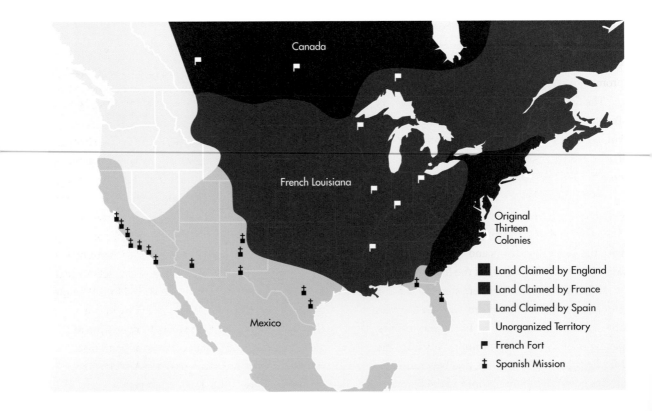

Canada

French Louisiana

Mexico

Original Thirteen Colonies

■ Land Claimed by England
■ Land Claimed by France
　 Land Claimed by Spain
　 Unorganized Territory
⚑ French Fort
✝ Spanish Mission

Washington and wants to bust up the banking giants—is walking in the footsteps of great populist Texans who came before him: fellows like Governor Jim Hogg, who made it his life's mission to break the railroad monopoly that was strangling Texan farmers and merchants at the end of the 19th century.

My Scots-Irish ancestors knew something about the struggles of the common man as they made their way to Texas. Combative and cussedly independent, those Borderer clans left the British Isles, where only nobility could own land, in search of soil they could call their own. They were suspicious of authority and were a literate bunch, schooled by Presbyterian preachers. My great-great-great-granddad Hezekiah Balch (born in 1741) was a Princeton grad and went on to found the first college in Tennessee. My great-granddad Sam Y. Wyly (born in 1815) was a Princeton man, too, and he set up some of the first schools west of the Cumberland Gap.

The Scots-Irish first settled along the Eastern Seaboard and in Appalachia, but slowly and doggedly they moved south and west, to places like Louisiana, where I was born, and on into the vast rangelands, piney woods, and bottomlands of Texas, where they saw the promise of being the masters of their own destiny.

The Scots-Irish took naturally to the cause of Texan independence from Mexico, and their contrarian, populist spirit still burns in Texan hearts today. That spirit and fight are what made Manifest Destiny possible and gave shape to the USA as we know it. Those frontier folks had to whip the French Empire (1763) to open the way for the Louisiana Purchase. Then they whipped the English Empire, twice. Then, with the Texas Revolution and the Mexican-American War, they whipped the Spanish Empire.

Other waves of newcomers came to the Lone Star State in those early years, too: the Germans after 1848, then the Czechs, Poles, and Italians, paving the way for today's immigrants from the Middle East, Southeast Asia, and beyond. Their stories got woven in with those of the Spanish mis-

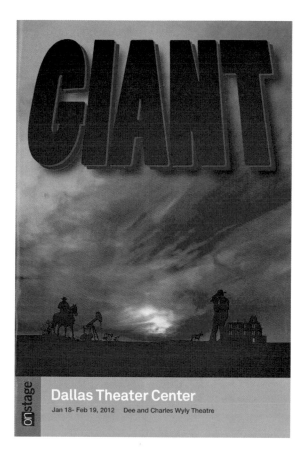

Signage for a 2012 production of *Giant* at the Wyly Theater in Dallas. When the movie version of *Giant* came out in 1956, its iconic story and imagery played a big part in making Sam Wyly want to move to Texas.

sionaries who'd come to Texas in the 1700s, shaping the land with their religious missions and *vaquero* traditions. Those Tejanos left their native Mexico behind and gave Texas the strong Hispanic imprint that is such a big part of our state's identity today.

About that "Texas identity"—well, it's something special. No other state in the union has anything like it. You're never going to hear people say, "Don't mess with Delaware!" or "Don't mess with Illinois!" When you put down roots in Texas, something in you changes, no matter where you're from or what religion or politics you practice. You're a Texan first, then a Mexican-American or Asian-American or Christian or Jew or liberal or conservative.

It started happening to me in 1956, when I came here for a summer job helping CPAs do audits in a hot tin warehouse, where I spent the day counting knives and forks before being "promoted" to an air-conditioned warehouse to count ladies' underwear. That was the year the movie *Giant* came out, and the images of Elizabeth Taylor and James Dean in the West Texas high desert made a big impression on me. So did the on-screen conflict between East Coast pretentiousness and the Texas wildcatter spirit. I knew I wanted to be a part of this place. So I finished my MBA in Ann Arbor, Michigan; got toughened up at a ninety-day boot camp at Lackland Air Force Base in San Antonio; and, while all my business-school buddies were snagging their first jobs at GM (the Facebook of the day), I got a job working for IBM in Fort Worth ("where the West begins").

When I finally broke out on my own in 1963, selling Fortran software services to petroleum engineers, my role models weren't computer geniuses. They were oil wildcatters, guys who were willing to drill fifty dry holes in the West Texas desert before they got a producing well. They never said die. And Texas bankers had faith and loaned them the money to do it! I knew that if I was going to hit it big—or

at least make enough for a mortgage, a car, and a house to put my family in—I was going to do it right here in Texas.

Hundreds of thousands of people from every race and walk of life are fleeing states like California, Illinois, and New York to start a new life in Texas. We've got some of the fastest-growing, and fastest-diversifying, metro areas in the country. That old abbreviation *GTT*, "gone to Texas" (coined back in the 19th century when hard-up farmers in Tennessee were heading to Texas in droves), has new currency today.

And we are welcoming our new neighbors with open arms. Because that's how Texans were brought up, sure, but also because we know that diversity and population growth are good for our state. Today Fort Worth, Dallas, Austin, and Houston are magnets for the "reverse migration" of African-Americans who are leaving behind the old urban enclaves of the Rust Belt, the Northeast, and the Left Coast. And most Texans know that the idea of a border fence along the

Two paintings by the artist David Wright, from left to right: Sam Wyly's great-great-great-granddad Hezekiah Balch; James Wyly, who fought the French and the Indians on the 1760s frontier and left land in North Carolina and Virginia to his children.

Rio Grande—aka the Rio Bravo, if you live on the Mexico side—is ludicrous. Why cut off all those good businesses and friendships that have driven life in our bustling border towns for years? And anyhow, we are all immigrants here if you go back a few generations—that is, unless you're a Cherokee or Choctaw or Comanche. And heck, the Cherokee were newcomers here, too, when they pushed aside the Waco Indians around 1830.

I'll be the first to say, and proudly, that Texas is cowboy country. Ranching is still a big deal here, and rodeos, too. But we've got a lot more than bronc riders down here. We've got the fastest-growing tech capital in the country; we're home to the best independent live-music showcase in the world; and out west in the little town of Marfa, where *Giant* was filmed all those years ago, we've got a contemporary-art scene like no other on earth.

Contrary to what some outsiders think, Texans are not obsessed with money. We're just good at earning, investing, and spending it. And we've got legislators and other public officials who know that the best thing they can do for the well-being of their state is to remove obstacles to building good companies that can generate wealth to go around. Our state lawmakers hold down full-time jobs outside the statehouse—as shop owners, ranchers, veterinarians, you name it. They know the true meaning of "business-friendly." And anyhow, lots of well-off Texans I know got into business for the thrill of the game. Dollars are just a way of keeping score. Most of us go to church on Sundays and read the high school football scores in the *Dallas Morning News* on Saturdays, and we go to dance halls like Billy Bob's on Saturday night.

Texas is the most American of all the big states. Liberty and freedom are rooted deep in our souls. We've got a strong independent, secessionist streak, and we've spilled blood to achieve self-determination. We're a melting pot in the truest sense of the term: We come here from all over, from all cultures, and we become

Texans. We have an egalitarian sense of justice, and our spirit is infused with the romance of the frontier. We like wide-open spaces, and we're not afraid to speak our minds. And we get things done. In California, if somebody sees a rattlesnake, he calls a committee meeting to discuss what to do about the rattlesnake problem. A Texan just kills the rattlesnake.

My son, Andrew, and I decided to write this book because we saw America being pulled in two very different directions. On one side was California, where taxation and regulation were squeezing the blood right out of entrepreneurs and sending that once-proud state to the very bottom of almost every major entrepreneurial ranking—right down there with California's overtaxed partners in misery, Illinois and New York. Leading America in the other direction is Texas, where smart regulation, low taxes, right-to-work laws, and tort reform are freeing entrepreneurs to invest, take risks, and grow—placing Texas at the very top of those same business and job-growth rankings, year after year.

The best and the brightest people and greatest companies are voting with their feet, abandoning the Rust Belt and the now-dysfunctional Golden State in unprecedented numbers to set up shop in Texas. What they find when they get here is lots of affordable housing, a low cost of living, and thriving local markets driven by everything from consumer tech to agriculture to clean energy. They also find fewer obstacles to building a career or a business than in any other big states. Andrew and I see in Texas a model for the other states and for Washington to follow. That Place on the Potomac needs to shrink itself and be less of a burden on Texans and the other folks in America who work for a living.

Today, political, economic, and cultural influence in this country is shifting south, away from its traditional seats of power in the Northeast and on the Left Coast. For us the reason is as clear as day: California, New York, and Illinois Got It Wrong. Texas Got It Right.

"Appomattox determined that the North would establish the rules for our Union ... for the next hundred years. The North would set the freight rates so damaging to the South. The North would determine the tariffs that made it so rich and kept the South so poor. The North would determine everything, it seemed, and would do so perpetually. But look at the situation today. Where is the power flowing? Always to the South. Where are the seats in Congress coming? To Texas and Florida. Where would you like to live if you were young and active and hopeful? Vermont? Or the Sunbelt?"

—James Michener, *Texas*, 1985

MOVING SOUTH

As new jobs and prosperity have driven population growth in the state, Texas's legislative and electoral oomph have grown right along with it. In fact, the Lone Star State is at the center of a slow, steady shift in the political landscape of the United States. Since 1940, seventy-nine congressional seats have drifted from the Midwest and the Northeast to the South and the West—and about 18 percent of those seats now belong to Texas, whose congressional delegation has grown for the past seven consecutive decades. The picture in the Electoral College, whose delegates send a candidate to the White House every four years, is similarly striking. The 2010 Census awarded Texas 38 electors, four more than it possessed after the 2000 count, and the most gained by any state. Meanwhile, the electoral clout of Rust Belt and Northeast power centers like Illinois, New York, and Pennsylvania is declining, and California has flatlined.

Change in House of Representatives Seats, 1960–2010

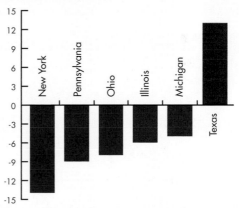

2010 Gains and Losses in Congress

Circles are sized by number that will be in the House

1   5   20

Colors show gains and losses

● Gain
● Same
● Loss

WE WERE BORN FIGHTING

COME AND TAKE IT.

When the early Texans revolted against Mexican rule and gave birth to a new nation, the Republic of Texas, it was a do-it-yourself thing. It all started with an old cannon, a homemade flag, and a cocky motto that's as resonant today as it was in October 1835. That's when colonists in a settlement named Gonzales decided to fight the one hundred troops that Mexico's dictator, General Santa Anna, had sent to take possession of the town's single rusting cannon. Oddly enough, that gun— the "It" in "Come and Take It"—had originally been sent from Mexico to help the Anglo colonists fight the Comanche Indians, who had wiped out San Saba and other Spanish missions. In fact, it was the Mexican regime that had invited those Anglo settlers to the Texas territories in the first place, as a defense against Indian raids. But times had changed. The dictator who had overthrown Mexico's democratic government now wanted to rule the "unruly" Texans.

The defenders of Gonzales rallied under the crude flag above, which was hastily made from the silk of a local gal's wedding dress. After a brief battle, the first of the Texas Revolution, the people of Gonzales kept their cannon. But the skirmish wasn't really about the gun (the thing barely worked). It was about defending local self-government from distant, centralized power— a notion that's as dear to Texans today as it was to the Gonzales guys in 1835. And just like your typical present-day Texan, those grassroots rebels knew the value of fighting words. "Come and Take It." You couldn't pay an ad agency a monster fee to come up with a better slogan than that.

...AND WE'VE NEVER STOPPED

The Battle of Gonzales (see opposite page) in October 1835 may have provided the spark for the Texas Revolution, but the settlers who won it probably didn't anticipate just how hot the flames of their new war would burn. By early the next year, six thousand Mexican troops had poured into Texas to put down the insurrection. Mexico's dictator, General Santa Anna—who in early 1835 had ransacked the Mexican silver-mining town of Zacatecas to crush the rebels who were fighting to preserve their freedom under the Mexican Constitution of 1824—issued a decree to his troops to take no prisoners. Five months after the rebels at Gonzales rallied under the slogan "Come and Take It," 187 of their brethren (including nine Tejanos, or Texans of Mexican descent) met their end at the point of a bayonet or barrel of a gun, fighting bitterly, to the last man and Bowie knife, at an old Spanish religious outpost called the Alamo. A few weeks later, Mexican troops massacred 342 Texan prisoners at Goliad, where an early version of the Texan Declaration of Independence had been signed. But the Texas rebels were not deterred. They'd thrown in all their chips with a perilous cause—that of independence from a dictatorship—and they were going to take that cause to its conclusion.

EVERY YEAR, TEXAS SCHOOLS TAKE SEVENTH-GRADE STUDENTS ON FIELD TRIPS TO THE ALAMO.

The Alamo, originally named Mission San Antonio de Valero, was a home to missionaries and their Indian converts for almost seven decades before it was secularized in 1793.

WE RALLY AROUND
THE FALLEN

After the massacres at the Alamo and Goliad (see previous pages) in 1836, Sam Houston's army was being pursued by General Santa Anna. Things were not looking good. Of course, that is exactly the kind of moment when a Texan likes to double down. Which is just what Sam Houston and his men did. Taking up positions in a forest next to the plain where Santa Anna and his troops had set up camp, Houston became the pursuer. On the afternoon of April 21, 1836, his Texans charged their enemy, shouting, "Remember the Alamo!" and "Remember Goliad!" The Battle of San Jacinto, as this fight came to be known, was over in eighteen minutes. Santa Anna's troops were

1824

routed, and he was taken prisoner. A month later he signed the Treaties of Velasco, which laid the foundation for Texan independence. The men of Sam Houston's army hadn't buried the memory of the Alamo and Goliad; they rallied around it. Those Texan fighters, whose democracy had been usurped by Santa Anna, knew in their hearts that to keep fighting was the only way forward.

Top: Uncle Alfred Wyly leads the charge in Charles Shaw's depiction of the Battle of San Jacinto. Above: A banner, based on the Mexican flag, that was flown during the Battle of the Alamo and afterward. The provinces of Zacatecas and Texas both rebelled when Santa Anna usurped their freedom, which had been guaranteed by the Mexican Constitution of 1824.

IN TEXAS, LAND AND LIVELIHOOD ARE
SACRED

What filled the empty expanses of early Texas with Scots-Irish and other migrant settlers wasn't just a hunger for land; it was a longing for the security and livelihood that land ownership brought to a family. The father of the Texas Republic, Stephen F. Austin, recognized that early on. So did Austin's cousin, Mary Austin Holley, who was so inspired by the magnanimous opportunity that Texas offered newcomers of every background that she wrote a book about the place in order to inspire more people to come here: *Texas, a History*, the first English-language chronicle of Texas, published in 1836. Three years later, Stephen Austin, as president of the young republic, pushed through a homestead act, which protected homesteaders from creditors who might seek to possess their land and property. The act also guaranteed every citizen or head of household "fifty acres or one town lot, including his or her homestead, and improvements not exceeding five hundred dollars in value." Similar provisions and protections have been enshrined in Texas's state constitution ever since. They've also guided Texas policy when it comes to property ownership—for example, protecting homeowners from overleveraging themselves to the banks by setting a commonsense minimum for down payments, a fact that helped steer Texas clear of the housing meltdown that triggered the Great Recession.

Top: The "Lone Star Flag" was adopted as the national flag of the Republic of Texas in 1839. Today it is the Texas state flag. Above: Mary Austin Holley.

THE PERKS OF NATIONHOOD

Texas is strong and self-sufficient by design. It is the only U.S. state to have joined the union by treaty—in 1845, when the sovereign Republic of Texas voted to join the union. Texas bargained hard with the federal government to win favorable terms and became unique among states by keeping full control of her public land. Texas also retained control of the republic's historic coastal waters, which extend three leagues (10.4 miles) from the coast instead of other states' one (3.5 miles). The rewards are tangible today. Oil, gas, and mineral leases on the state's public onshore and offshore territory have helped finance an enormous permanent public education endowment at both the K–12 and university levels, and Texas's extrawide coastal waters hold colossal renewable-energy potential. Independent energy producers operating in Texas currently hold leases for 4,000 megawatts of offshore wind capacity, enough to power 3.2 million homes. Once again, Texas proves that independence pays.

A 2012 *NEWSWEEK* RANKING NOTED THAT TEXAS HAS FIFTEEN OF THE BEST 100 PUBLIC HIGH SCHOOLS IN THE U.S.

Other States' Coastal Boundaries: 3.5 Miles

Texas's Coastal Boundaries: 10.4 Miles

Oil and Gas Revenues Generated in the Gulf Since 1922, Earmarked to Support K–12 Public Education Throughout Texas

$2.43 billion
What Texas gained from its extra two leagues of coastal land

$519.3 million
What Texas would have gotten if it were just a regular state

Texas Public Lands Reserved to Fund K–12 Education

13 million acres, almost twice the size of Massachusetts. Total contributions, 1922–2010: More than $13 billion

Texas Public Lands Reserved to Fund University Education

2.1 million acres, 144 times the size of Manhattan. Total contributions in 2011: $507 million

x 144

TEXAS GAME-CHANGER
SAM HOUSTON

"The hopes of the usurper were inspired by a belief that the citizens of Texas were disunited and divided in opinion, and that alone has been the cause of the present invasion of our rights. He shall realize the fallacy of his hopes, in the union of her citizens, and their Eternal Resistance to his plans against constitutional liberty. We will enjoy our birth-right, or perish in its defense."

—Sam Houston, in his Call to Arms of December 12, 1835

No single name is more revered in Texas than that of Sam Houston. Not because that name has been given to countless schools, libraries, and public spaces, and to our biggest city. No, Sam Houston is revered by Texans because the man deserves it. He led the Battle of San Jacinto, which won the Texas War of Independence. Then he became the first president of the fledgling Republic of Texas. Then, three years after his first term ended, he came back for a second, out of sheer love and duty. When the Lone Star Nation became a U.S. state, the people elected him senator. Then they elected him governor. And let's not forget that before Sam Houston became Texas's most famous Texan, he'd already started the first primary school in Tennessee (though he'd received little formal education of his own), been a congressman and governor for that state, fought against the mistreatment of Indians before Congress, and taken a bullet in the War of 1812.

The challenges Houston faced in life would certainly have been more than enough to take down almost any man. But Sam Houston was Scots-Irish to the core—indomitable, resolute, independent. As with many Americans of Scots-Irish decent, Houston's family history can be traced to Ulster, Ireland, then across the Atlantic to Pennsylvania, to the farms of the Shenandoah Valley, to Virginia, and later to the mountains of East Tennessee. His Presbyterian upbringing engendered in him a respect for the common man and for democratic ideals, and his early life acquainted him intimately with the value of hard physical work.

Abandoning a job at his family's store in Maryville, Tennessee, Houston left home at sixteen to live with the Cherokee Indians on an island in the Hiawassee River. To the Cherokees he was known as the Raven. He adopted their language, customs, and dress. Throughout his life, and especially in times of personal pain and uncertainty, Houston turned to his adopted family for support and guidance. His support for Indian nations put him in conflict with his mentor, Andrew Jackson, but Houston always held firm. "I am aware that in presenting myself as the advocate of the Indians and their rights," he proclaimed to Congress, "I shall stand very much alone." But standing alone was not something Houston feared.

That's probably a big part of what drew him to Texas in 1832. There was the lure of free land, sure, but there was also the promise of building a future unobstructed by conventional viewpoints and hierarchical political systems. Like so many others, Houston was immediately caught up in the enthusiasm of the Texas Revolution. Never hesitant to use strong words or to take up arms for a cause, Houston became commander-in-chief of the Army of Texas. In that capacity he issued his eloquent and effective Call to Arms against the Republic of Mexico in December 1835.

Years later, as a senator, Houston foresaw the cataclysm that would become the Civil War. He urged his fellow legislators to support the Compromise of 1850. In a stirring speech he invoked the scripture with the words "a nation divided against itself cannot stand." It wasn't until eight years later, as the nation hurtled toward the disaster Houston had tried to avert, that Abraham Lincoln made those words famous for posterity. In short, Houston was a man of arms who deemed keeping the peace the noblest deed of the mighty.

Opposite: Sam Houston circa 1861. This page, left: This flag was flown at a fort near Goliad before being destroyed during the massacre there. (Houston had initially ordered his troops to retreat, but he was not heeded until too late.) Right: The 576-foot-tall San Jacinto Monument is the world's tallest column, taller than the Washington Monument. Its 220-ton star commemorates the site of the Battle of San Jacinto.

★ LONE STAR ★
MANY NATIONS

In his 2011 book, *American Nations*, Colin Woodard makes the case that America's political and cultural landscape is not divided along red-state/blue-state or even regional geographic lines, but along generations-old cultural boundaries that can be traced to migration patterns and belief systems dating to the colonial era. Within those boundaries lie eleven "nations," each with its own distinctive set of values and political leanings. Out East you've got the cosmo-politan mercantile culture of the New Netherlands (originating with the Dutch settlements that would become New York City) and the Calvinist civic-mind-edness of Yankeedom. Farther down, you've got the caste-oriented plantation culture of the Deep South; out in the Rockies and beyond you've got the hard-bitten, government-wary culture of the Far West; and

so on. The frontiers where these nations meet can be fault lines that breed sectarian division. They can also make for dynamic convergences. Take a look at where Texas is on that map. Here, the brawling, independent-minded Scots-Irish of Greater Appalachia come up against the Quaker-influenced apple-pie Americanism of the Midlands and the deep-rooted democratizing forces of El Norte, a region of Spanish heritage rooted in the earliest missionary adventures in the New World. Encroaching from the southeast are the aristo-cratic ideals of the Deep South. It all makes for a heady mix—progressivism and libertarianism min-gling with old-school conservatism and even revolutionary sentiment—that has no equal in North America. Here, America's old fiefdoms blend to become something new, something purely Texan.

WE'RE A BONA FIDE
★ MELTING POT ★

EACH YEAR, ABOUT 83,000 IMMIGRANTS BECOME LEGAL PERMANENT RESIDENTS IN TEXAS.

The history of the early settlement of Texas is more a tale of migration than immigration—specifically the epic westward movement of Scots-Irish families from their beachheads in Appalachia. "They arrived in great numbers," wrote James Michener of these Borderer clans, in his book *Texas*, "filtering down the famed Natchez Trace from Pennsylvania, Ohio, Kentucky, and Tennessee. They were a resolute, courageous, self-driven, arrogant lot." The Scots-Irish set the feisty character of the republic and of the state that followed, but they were not the only European national group to shape the destiny of Texas. Starting in the 1840s, Germans came in droves too, establishing the town of Fredericksburg and creating a German-speaking belt that stretched across much of the state. Czechs and Poles soon followed. Those peoples managed to preserve their language and folkways for a generation or two, but soon enough Texas would change them. Carved from the bosom of Mexico, Texas gave rise to a hybrid culture like no other. That culture was self-selecting, drawing out the best traits of each group that settled here: the tolerant pluralism of northern European immigrants, the scrappy individualism of the Scots-Irish, the reformist drive of Hispanic Texans, and so on. The story continues today, as new groups, many from traditional immigrant hubs like California and New York, are absorbed into Texas's welcoming fold.

Fourth of July parade on Main Street, Fredericksburg, 1905.

OUR FRIENDS
IN NEED ARE FRIENDS INDEED

In the hours and days after Hurricane Katrina, as buses from New Orleans started rolling into Houston—which eventually took in some 240,000 people fleeing the storm's aftermath—word went out among staff at the city's hospitals and shelters that they should stop calling the newcomers "refugees" or even "evacuees," but rather "guest citizens." It was a quintessentially Texan gesture, and it grew from the understanding that extending hospitality means more than an offer of food and shelter. It means honoring the innate human dignity of those you're helping. Is it any wonder that 150,000 of those former Louisianans eventually decided to lay down roots and become Texans? And proud, productive Texans at that. You could say

TO ACCOMMODATE KATRINA EVACUEES, THE ASTRODOME CANCELED ALL EVENTS THROUGH DECEMBER 2005.

Welcome to Texas

Drive Friendly-The Texas Way

12,000+ QUILTS FOR EVACUEES!

that this kind of hospitality is just in our DNA, and you'd be right, but Texans' attitude toward outsiders and newcomers goes even deeper than good manners and good works. Really, it comes down to a basic belief shared by millions of Texans that a big tent and open arms make for a more dynamic and prosperous place.

Left: After Hurricane Katrina, the Houston Astrodome was a haven for those displaced by the storm. Five years later, not even Houston mayor Annise Parker knew how many storm victims were still living in the city. "I don't know what the number is, and I don't believe we will ever know, nor should we need it any longer. They are Houstonians." Top: Road signs like this one can be found at every entry point to Texas. Above: A sign at the George Brown Convention Center in Houston touts the large number of quilts being provided for Katrina evacuees.

OUR BOOTS
ALWAYS FIT

There's something about the Lone Star State that just gets under your skin, no matter where you come from or what you believe. If you live here long enough, eventually you're going to stop thinking of yourself as a Texan Jew or Christian or Muslim and start thinking of yourself as a Jewish or Christian or Muslim Texan. And it won't be long before you go out and buy yourself a pair of cowboy boots. They are the reigning symbol of Texas culture for good reason: Cowboy boots are how we tell the world we're Texan, and they're also how we express ourselves. Walk into almost any boot store in the

state and you'll see hundreds if not thousands of designs and patterns and styles—and if you don't see something you like, there are plenty of custom boot makers who will craft a pair just for you. It's only appropriate that the father of custom cowboy boot–making in Texas was an immigrant, a Sicilian named Salvatore Lucchese. He and his sons and grandsons have made boots by hand in their El Paso workshop for everyone from Teddy Roosevelt to LBJ to Francisco Madero, the leader of the revolution that brought democracy to Mexico in the early 20th century.

Opposite: Lucchese released 125 pairs of these special boots, which retailed for $12,500, to celebrate its 125th anniversary. This page, clockwise from top: The Alamo Plaza Lucchese Building in the 1940s; these custom-made cowboy boots, created by a craftsman at the Justin Boot Co., were featured on the cover of 2007's *Lone Stars of David: The Jews of Texas;* Zsa Zsa Gabor gets fitted for Lucchese boots in the 1950s.

WE'RE BORN
★ DEAL MAKERS ★

facility for political power brokering early in life, when as a student at the University of Texas he volunteered for Lyndon Johnson's first congressional campaign. At the 1976 Democratic National Convention he accomplished what had been thought impossible: bringing together the arch-conservative George Wallace and the arch-liberal George McGovern. Strauss cajoled both into standing at the dais alongside the Democrats' newly anointed presidential candidate, Jimmy Carter, for the TV and newspaper cameras.

"While his power derived from being a friend to the White House and a force on the Hill," wrote Strauss's niece Kathryn McGarr in her 2011 biography of him, "those relationships all came down to his personality—the sparkle in his eye, his enormous and endearing ego, his humor and his colorful way of speaking 'Texan'…." That is to say, cussin', an art Strauss had mastered, though he is said to have reined it in, at least a little, when Bush named him ambassador to the Soviet Union. That was a president's most important and delicate ambassadorial appointment in those days. And it was a job made for a Texan.

Former First Lady Barbara Bush used to call Bob Strauss, the legendary Democratic Party insider who became Bush I's ambassador to Russia, "everybody's friend." She also said that he "could sell you the paper off your own wall." As a fellow Texan, she was paying Strauss a high compliment, because there are few things we value more in the Lone Star State than the fine art of persuasion. Strauss—who served as the chairman of the Democratic Party during the Nixon-Ford years and cofounded one of the biggest law firms in the world—was born in Lockhart, Texas, to Jewish German immigrant parents who ran a general store. He discovered his

Strauss makes his point in 1972. That same year, in the wake of George McGovern's loss to President Nixon, Strauss was elected chairman of the Democratic National Committee.

★ WE CAN BRING DOWN ★
EMPIRES

"He was a rascal, but our rascal." That's how Mayor Jack Gordon of Lufkin, Texas, described Charlie Wilson to the *New York Times* after the hard-partying congressman's death in 2010. One of the commanders of the destroyer Wilson served on during his stint in the Navy in the 1950s dubbed him "the best officer on ship but the worst in port." When Wilson was just a teenager, he won his first political skirmish by using his learner's permit to drive black voters to the polls in his hometown of Trinity, Texas, so they could vote against his next-door neighbor, city councilman Charles Hazard, who'd killed Wilson's dog. As a cadet at the Annapolis Naval Academy, Wilson earned more demerits than any other student in the history of the institution. And as a representative for Texas's second district, which includes Lufkin, he utterly failed to emulate his Bible Belt constituents' church-going ways, but they sent him back to Washington 11 times anyhow, because he knew how to serve his district. Probably the most talented horse-trader in Congress, Wilson scored major wins for East Texas, including the establishment of Big Thicket National Preserve and a brand-new Veterans Hospital in Lufkin. But he was more famous for how he served his country: In the 1980s, Wilson succeeded in significantly upping the funding for military support of anti-Communist forces in Soviet-occupied Afghanistan. The CIA loved him for that and made him the only civilian in history to receive the agency's Honored Colleague Award. The support Wilson won for the Afghan freedom fighters ultimately won the war. In 1989 the Soviets finally called it quits and pulled out of the country, an act that was the nail in the coffin of the Soviet empire, which fell just two years later. When asked by *60 Minutes* in 1988 to explain the imminent demise of the Soviets in neighboring Afghanistan, the former president of Pakistan, Mohammad Zia ul-Haq, put his answer in the simplest possible terms: "Charlie did it."

Wilson, pictured here in Afghanistan in 1987, had a spot on the House Defense Appropriations Committee, which allowed him to direct funds to support mujahideen efforts.

WE PRIZE THE ART OF PERSUASION

It was called the Treatment, and it has become as much a part of Lyndon Baines Johnson's legacy as the Great Society, civil rights, and the Vietnam War. Here's how the reporters Rowland Evans and Robert Novak described it in their book about the thirty-sixth president: "He moved in close, his face a scant millimeter from his target, his eyes widening and narrowing, his eyebrows rising and falling. From his pockets poured clippings, memos, statistics. Mimicry, humor, and genius of analogy made the Treatment an almost hypnotic experience and rendered the target stunned and helpless."

You could disagree with the particular causes that LBJ was advancing, but you couldn't help but admire the way he got his point across. In the end, this son of the Texas Hill Country was such a persuasive arguer not because he was a bully or a browbeater, but because he was a true believer. He was married to his causes and sure of their rightness, and woe be to those who didn't see the light. More than his famously enormous appetites and ambitions, it was that conviction, that rock-solid faith in his choices, that made LBJ so Texan.

LBJ gets up close and personal with Georgia senator Richard Russell, 1963.

...AND WE'RE NOT AFRAID TO

SPEAK OUR MINDS

"Carter is a dead chicken around John Hill's neck."

—Bill Clements

Texans love an underdog, and they really love a bulldog. They got both in Bill Clements, the ex–oil field roughneck who in 1979 became the first Republican governor of the state of Texas since Reconstruction. Texans also love a visionary, and Clements was a man who had no problem following his instincts into uncharted territory. He unabashedly identified himself as a self-made millionaire, and in a strategy that almost sounds old-hat in our era, the upstart candidate in 1978 laid out a simple plan to beat his accustomed-to-winning Democratic opponent, John Hill. Firstly Clements said, he would outspend Hill. Secondly he would wrap President Jimmy Carter around the Democrat's neck like a "dead chicken." His gamble worked, as did his strategy of playing to independent and rural voters.

Underpinning Clements's public life was an abiding belief that Texas was a state like no other, a de facto nation within a nation. Though he'd done his time in Washington, he spoke his mind like the native son that he was, and Texans rewarded him for it. When Clements lost his re-election bid to Democrat Mark White in 1982, he said, true to form, "Hell, I've

drilled dry holes before." Midway through White's term, bumper stickers started appearing around the state that said, "Gee, I miss Gov. Clements." In 1986, Clements swept White out of office and began a second term. As his longtime aide George Bayoud put it, "I still hear people say, 'I didn't always agree with Bill Clements, but I sure miss the way he used to say it.'"

> **CLEMENTS GAVE $100 MILLION TO SOUTHWESTERN MEDICAL CENTER, THE LARGEST CIVIC DONATION IN DALLAS HISTORY.**

Clements in his Dallas office, 1978

ON MAY 29, 1992, AFTER INSTITUTING THE TEXAS LOTTO, GOVERNOR RICHARDS BOUGHT THE FIRST SCRATCH-OFF TICKET.

OUR POLITICIANS HAVE GOT
CHARACTER TO SPARE

Ann Richards knew how to make a big impression while making you think she wasn't even trying. When she was still the state treasurer of Texas, she gave the keynote address at the 1988 Democratic National Convention and brought the house down with her wit and candor. "If you give us the chance," she said of women political leaders, "we can perform. After all, Ginger Rogers did everything that Fred Astaire did. She just did it backwards and in high heels." After she became governor, Richards decided that for her sixtieth birthday she was going to learn to ride a Harley, so she practiced in the parking lot of the Department of Public Safety and got her license. But she was a serious trailblazer, too. Nearly half of the appointments she made as governor were women, and a record number were black and Hispanic.

"She's a person who never stopped enjoying whatever there was in life she could enjoy," said Kay Bailey Hutchison, who succeeded Richards as state treasurer and went on to blaze a few trails herself. A daughter of La Marque, Texas, Hutchison was a small-town prom queen and a UT cheerleader, something she's always been proud of, even after becoming the first woman sent by Texas voters to the U.S. Senate, where as of 2012, she was the longest-serving female member. She was also the first female news-caster to appear on TV in Houston, and she has served as chair of the Board of Visitors at West Point. She also happens to be the first Texas senator to receive more than 4 million votes in a single election. She's a Republican, and a great asset to her party, but she votes her conscience over the party line, whether the issue is abortion or health-care reform. Hutchison's accomplishments earned her a place in the *Ladies' Home Journal* ranking of the "Top 30 Most Powerful Women in America" in 2001. Like Richards, Hutchison is admired by liberals and conservatives alike in Texas, a fact that illustrates a long-standing truth about Texans: We like to vote for the person, not the party.

HUTCHISON'S GREAT-GREAT-GRANDFATHER, CHARLES S. TAYLOR, SIGNED THE TEXAS DECLARATION OF INDEPENDENCE.

Opposite: When she was nearly 60, Richards started riding a Harley-Davidson motorcycle because, she said, "I thought I needed to do something kind of jazzy." This page: Hutchison cheers before the start of play during a Texas Rangers baseball game, 2011.

LAWMAKERS WHO REALLY

Meet a Few of Our State Legislators

Alma Allen

District 131, Democrat,
2005–Present
Retired teacher, principal,
and professor. Currently an
educational consultant.

Charles "Doc" Anderson

District 56, Republican,
2005–Present
Small-animal veterinarian
for the past thirty years.
Raises cattle.

Cindy Burkett

District 101, Republican,
2011–Present
Owner of five Subway
sandwich shops.

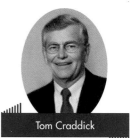

Tom Craddick

District 82, Republican,
1993–Present
Sales representative for
Mustang Mud, an oil-field
supply company.

Charlie Geren

District 99, Republican,
2001–Present
Owner of Railhead
Smokehouse Restaurant.

Patricia Harless

District 126, Republican,
2007–Present
Owner of a used-car
dealership in Houston.

Mark Homer

District 3, Democrat,
1999–2010
Owner of several
Sonic Drive-In restaurants.

Armando "Mando" Martinez

District 39, Democrat,
2005–Present
Firefighter and paramedic
with the City of Weslaco
Fire Department.

Sid Miller

District 59, Republican,
2001–Present
Rancher, rodeo participant,
and world-record calf-roper.

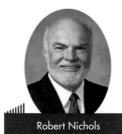

Robert Nichols

District 3, Republican,
2007–Present
Plastics-manufacturing
engineer; holds thirty-two
U.S. patents.

Debbie Riddle

District 150, Republican,
2003–Present
Horse breeder and owner
of R&R Horse Farms.

KNOW MAIN STREET

State legislators in Texas aren't professional politicians. They are veterinarians, used-car dealers, firefighters, ranchers, and main-street entrepreneurs of many kinds, from fast-food franchisee to air-conditioning repairman. The Texas legislature is designed that way: The reps' salaries are kept low, and the regular session is just 140 days every other year, creating one of the leanest, most efficient state-lawmaking bodies in the country. In 2011, a state lawmaker in Texas was paid $7,200 per year, plus a per diem of $150 for each of the 140 days the legislature is in session. By contrast, California paid its legislators $95,291 per year, and a whopping 80 percent of that state's representatives listed "full-time legislator" as their occupation. Virtually no member of the Texas statehouse did the same.

Annual Salaries for State Legislators in the Eight Largest States

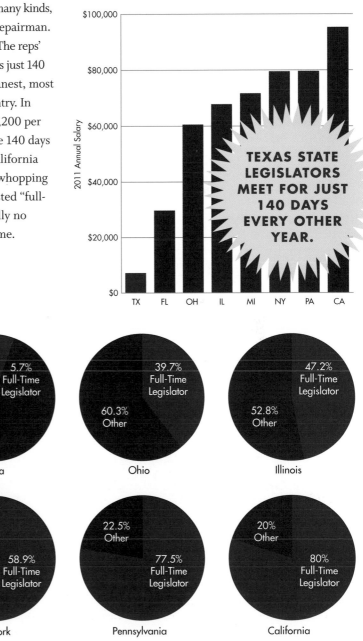

TEXAS STATE LEGISLATORS MEET FOR JUST 140 DAYS EVERY OTHER YEAR.

Officially Listed Occupations of State Legislators

Texas
- 1.7% Full-Time Legislator
- 98.3% Other

Florida
- 5.7% Full-Time Legislator
- 94.3% Other

Ohio
- 39.7% Full-Time Legislator
- 60.3% Other

Illinois
- 47.2% Full-Time Legislator
- 52.8% Other

Michigan
- 43.5% Other
- 56.5% Full-Time Legislator

New York
- 41.1% Other
- 58.9% Full-Time Legislator

Pennsylvania
- 22.5% Other
- 77.5% Full-Time Legislator

California
- 20% Other
- 80% Full-Time Legislator

LEADING THE RIGHT-TO-WORK
REVOLUTION

U.S. AUTOMOBILE-PLANT OPENINGS
AND CLOSINGS, 1994–2012

MAJOR PLANT CLOSINGS

Year	Manufacturer	Location	Jobs Lost
1994	General Motors	Pontiac, MI	1,800
1996	General Motors	Sleepy Hollow, NY	3,450
1999	General Motors	Flint, MI	1,200
2004	Ford	Edison, NJ	900
2005	Ford	Baltimore, MD	1,100
2005	General Motors	Lansing, MI	1,600
2005	General Motors	Linden, NJ	1,100
2005	General Motors	Lorain, OH	1,700
2006	Ford	Hapeville, GA	1,950
2006	Ford	Hazelwood, MO	1,445
2006	General Motors	Oklahoma City, OK	2,200
2007	Ford	Mishawaka, IN	250
2007	Ford	Norfolk, VA	2,200
2007	Hummer	Wixom, MI	1,560
2008	Chrysler LLC	Doraville, GA	1,500
2008	General Motors	Fenton, MO	1,700
2008	General Motors	Janesville, WI	2,200
2008	General Motors	Moraine, OH	2,500
2009	Chrysler LLC	Fenton, MO	2,400
2009	Chrysler LLC	Newark, DE	2,100
2009	General Motors	Pontiac, MI	1,100
2009	General Motors	Spring Hill, TN	2,500
2009	General Motors	Wilmington, DE	655
2010	Nummi	Fremont, CA	4,700
2011	Ford	St. Paul, MN	800
2012	General Motors	Shreveport, LA	950

MAJOR PLANT OPENINGS

Year	Manufacturer	Location	Employees
1994	BMW	Greer, SC	4,900
1996	Toyota	Buffalo, WV	1,054
1996	Toyota	Princeton, IN	4,300
1997	Nissan	Decherd, TN	850
1997	Mercedes-Benz	Vance, AL	4,500
2001	Toyota	Huntsville, AL	860
2001	Honda	Lincoln, AL	4,000
2003	Nissan	Canton, MI	3,400
2003	Toyota	San Antonio, TX	2,800
2005	Hyundai	Montgomery, AL	2,700
2007	Toyota/Subaru	Lafayette, IN	1,230
2008	Honda	Greensburg, IN	2,000
2010	Toyota	Blue Springs, MS	2,000
2010	Kia	West Point, GA	2,500
2011	Volkswagen	Chattanooga, TN	2,700

4,700

2,200

2,800

Texas was one of the first U.S. states to pass right-to-work legislation, which prohibits compulsory union membership and protects nonunion workers against employment discrimination. It turns out that this isn't just good democratic practice; it's good for business. Nowhere is the proof of this fact more striking than in the auto industry. Car manufacturers are building more of their new plants in right-to-work territory and shuttering them in closed-shop states, which is causing the industry as a whole to migrate slowly out of the heavily unionized Rust Belt and into the South. What's more, all those migrating auto jobs are proving to be strong stimulants to the economies of right-to-work states. To put it simply, the Texas model works. And it's the right way to protect workers. The principle is laid out plain and simple in Texas's labor statute: "The right to work is the right to live."

TEXAS IS HOME TO 479 AUTO MANUFACTURING FIRMS, EMPLOYING 33,000 WORKERS.

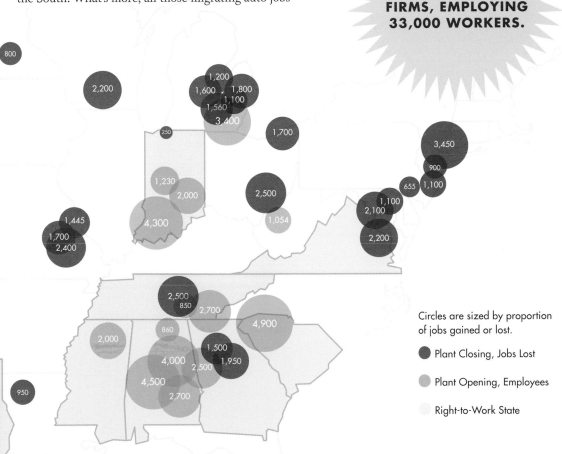

Circles are sized by proportion of jobs gained or lost.

● Plant Closing, Jobs Lost

● Plant Opening, Employees

○ Right-to-Work State

THE CONVENIENCE STORE

WAS BORN HERE

It gets hot in Texas. That's why Texans opened ice houses, stores where folks would get blocks of ice to take home to put in their icebox. In the 1920s, a man named Joe C. Thompson was working in one of those ice houses, the Southland Ice Company in Dallas, when he had a bright idea: Why not sell milk, eggs, and other perishables along with all that ice? After all, he already had the means to keep the stuff cold. Ice-house customers and other passersby cottoned to the idea, and Thompson's side operation took off. After a few years he changed the store's name to Tote'm—as in, buy the things you need and tote 'em home. In 1945 he changed it again, to 7-Eleven, because he was open from 7 a.m. to 11 p.m.—a whole lot longer than your typical grocery store. Today, the franchise chain Thompson started operates more than 46,000 outlets worldwide, having outstripped McDonald's in 2007 as the world's largest chain store.

The first 7-Eleven was located at the corner of Edgefield and 12th Street in the Oak Cliff section of Dallas.

The most compelling origin story for the hamburger is the one given by the Texas historian Francis X. Tolbert. He holds that one Fletcher Davis served ground-beef sandwiches at his Athens, Texas, café as early as the 1880s, and in 1904 famously introduced them to the wider public at the St. Louis World's Fair. Texans love a good burger, and a big one, and they like it their way. And while McDonald's gets credit for popularizing the hamburger on a global scale, our own Whataburger chain—which includes some 700 locations in Texas and across the South— stands as a testament to the happiest possible marriage of smart entrepreneurship, family-business values, targeted marketing, and great fast food. The first Whataburger stand went up in Corpus Christi in 1950,

serving five-inch-wide Texas-size burgers made from 100 percent fresh-never-frozen USDA-inspected beef. Each sandwich was made to order and customized on demand to suit any customer's taste. That's still the M.O. of the company, which is now run by Tom Dobson, the son of its founder. Nowadays Whataburger has a cult following among Texans, who love the chain for sticking adamantly to its regional roots.

...AND SO WAS THE WORLD'S BEST BURGER

An entrepreneur named Harmon Dobson

HELL AND HIGH WATER
DON'T STOP US

Until the late 19th century, before the cattle and oil booms forever altered the face of the land, Texas was not an easy place to get around. The state was a landscape of dirt farms and river-bottom plantations connected by crude wagon trails. "It was difficult enough to get goods ashore in Texas, but it became a nightmare to move freight overland," writes the historian T. R. Fehrenbach in *Lone Star: A History of Texas and the Texans*. "Only a few miles of roadway in the entire state in 1860 were graded; exactly twenty miles in all was planked or similarly improved." What's more, railroads came pretty late to Texas; the first spikes weren't driven until 1852. For one thing, there just weren't any big cities yet in Texas for the rails to connect together.

This meant that overland travel across the vast state was usually of the hoof-powered variety—like the stagecoach pictured above, which carried mail between the towns of Plano and Bonham. Even in the best of weather, it was slow going. "The bogs of old Ireland could never compare to the Texan mud," wrote an Irish nun to a sister back home in 1851, describing her journey by mule-drawn coach from Galveston to San Antonio. And yet those early stage lines were logistical marvels of their day, operating on pinpoint timetables that depended on long-distance communication and quick, efficient turnaround at the staging stops, during which mule and horse teams were swapped out, repairs made, and cargo unloaded.

Mud and potholes couldn't hold Texans back for long, especially when there were fortunes to be made in lumber, cotton, cattle, and, later, oil—all of which had to get from source to market in staggering quantities, and fast. First the railroads came, then the motor coaches and the roads they traveled on, then the great container ports of Galveston and Houston (see pages 48, 54), then the airports—including Dallas–Fort Worth's, the biggest in the country. Simply put, Texans got very good, very quickly, at linking distant points on a map—and even off the map (see opposite page).

TEXANS
AIM HIGH

"What was once the furthest outpost on the old frontier of the West will be the furthest outpost on the new frontier of science and space."

—John Fitzgerald Kennedy

The thirty-fifth president pronounced those words to Rice University students in September 1962, just after the start of construction of a sprawling new aerospace facility on a patch of undeveloped land near Galveston Bay. The name of this new NASA outpost, intended to replace an earlier one in Langley, Virginia, was the Manned Spacecraft Center, though most everyone would come to know it as Mission Control—or simply as "Houston." That two-syllable call sign has held a lot of power for the crews of the 166 manned vehicles that Mission Control has guided to the heavens and back over the years. "Houston": It is the salutation that begins every communication from space to earth. It is the astronauts' tether to all things terrestrial, to native dirt, to the place where they train and live.

It was a Texas senator named Lyndon Johnson who was the staunchest supporter of the legislation that created NASA in 1958, but the fact that his home state was chosen as the nerve center of all human spaceflight in America was a matter of practicality. Houston had it all: advanced telecommunications networks, all-weather airports, excellent ports, a huge pool of skilled contractors and engineers, and a built-in brain trust supplied by the University of Houston and Rice University. And then there was the fact that Texans, who in a mere hundred years had transformed their state from a dirt-road backwater into a global transportation and communications hub, knew a little something about shooting the moon.

Neil Armstrong and Edwin "Buzz" Aldrin prepare to move a passive seismometer (used to record moonquakes) during a practice session for the Apollo 11 lunar mission at the Manned Spacecraft Center in Houston.

OUR BIG SNAGS GET
BIG SOLUTIONS

No single man did more to clear the way for the Lone Star State's ascendance as a great shipping powerhouse than the legendary riverboat captain Henry Miller Shreve. It all had to do with a logjam, a very nasty one in the Red River that started in southern Louisiana and continued upstream for more than a hundred miles, clogging routes deep into the river's Texas watershed. So immense, so seemingly impenetrable, was this ancient "snag" of driftwood and debris that it had earned its own name: the Great Raft. In 1832 the U.S. government assigned Captain Shreve to bust up the Great Raft. Ten years later, using flat-bottomed crafts of his own design called "snag boats" (that's one

pictured above), he'd cleared more than seventy miles of the Red River, partially freeing up the immense watershed. That was awfully good news for Texan cotton growers, who desperately needed a faster way to get their product to market in New Orleans.

Shreve's feat had a couple of immediate side effects: It caused so much water to empty out of the Red River watershed that steamboat depots upstream suddenly found themselves dry. That allowed other river towns to pick up the slack and thrive. A backwater settlement called Dallas was one of those lucky towns. Shreve also proved that through sheer sweat and gumption, even Texas—a land of shallow, barely navigable rivers emptying into reef-obstructed bays—could turn its native waters into major throughways for trade.

If you care to see proof, take a cruise along Texas's Gulf Coast and behold the vast web of waterborne commerce that converges there. Those 350 or so miles of waterfront now harbor no fewer than ten bustling deep-water container ports, from Galveston to Brownsville to Corpus Christi to Port Arthur to the granddaddy of them all, Houston, which today is the busiest port in the United States in terms of foreign tonnage. The Port of Houston also serves as the gateway to a feat of engineering at least as impressive as Captain Shreve's: the Houston Ship Channel (pictured below), a fifty-mile-long, forty-five-foot-deep waterway carved from the Buffalo Bayou and Galveston Bay. The channel, lined with freighter berths, container terminals, and public and private docks, is a city unto itself. Today the Port of Houston leads the country in tonnage for all kinds of import and export commodities (see page 54).

All together, the ports of Texas sustain a million jobs that generate $48 billion of personal income each year. They comprise a thousand miles of channel, all maintained by the Army Corps of Engineers, and they receive and ship hundreds of millions of tons of cargo annually, from Volkswagens (most of those sold in the U.S. pass through the Port of Houston) to Midwestern grain to wood pulp and steel pipe. That's a far cry from the days of Captain Shreve and his snag boats. But really, what Shreve did wasn't any different from what later champions of Texas's waterways have done: open a gateway to the world and let prosperity flow in.

THE HOUSTON SHIP CHANNEL WAS DESIGNATED A NATIONAL CIVIL ENGINEERING LANDMARK IN 1987.

TEXANS ARE TRUE
TRAILBLAZERS

There is little that can stand between a Texan entrepreneur and a market for his goods. In the latter half of the 19th century, as demand for beef soared in the great cities of the North, the cow herders of the Texas borderlands looked at the hundreds of miles of perilous territory that separated them from those hungry cities and said, "We can do this." Thus began the era of the great cattle drives, which delivered some 5 million animals from Texas to the North in the decade and a half after the Civil War. "The wild Texas cattle were not modern pasture steers," writes the Texas historian T. R. Fehrenbach: "They could walk to market, over thousands of miles, across rivers and sands, through blazing droughts and Indian raids. They made their own roads, along the fringelands on the open plains." The most hard-traveled of those roads—like the Chisolm Trail, which began deep in Texas and ended at railheads in Kansas—became legend. And the exploits of the trail drivers soon became legend as well, laying the very foundation of cowboy mythology. And sure, a few of those trail riders were gunslingers and adventurers, but we should never forget that the Texas cowboy was, first and foremost, a businessman.

AMERICA'S TRADE NEXUS

More goods are exported to the world through Texas than through any other state, and no other state has more highways, airports, and railways to carry all that freight. Our overland routes—including I-35 and I-10, two of the busiest trucking corridors in the country—carried $87 billion worth of goods to Mexico alone in 2011 and received another $93 billion worth of goods coming north. Our 1,254 miles of frontier with Mexico have always positioned Texas as the dominant trade partner with our neighbor to the south. Nearly 3 million trucks a year pass through Texas's forty-five border crossings—that's more international entry gateways than any other state. One eighteen-wheeler crosses the Laredo World Trade Bridge every thirty seconds. Without Texas, America's annual trade volume would plummet by $250 billion.

Texas at the Crossroads

Positioned at the intersection of I-10 and I-35, Texas sits at the center of a trade circle that covers most of Mexico and reaches deep into the American heartland.

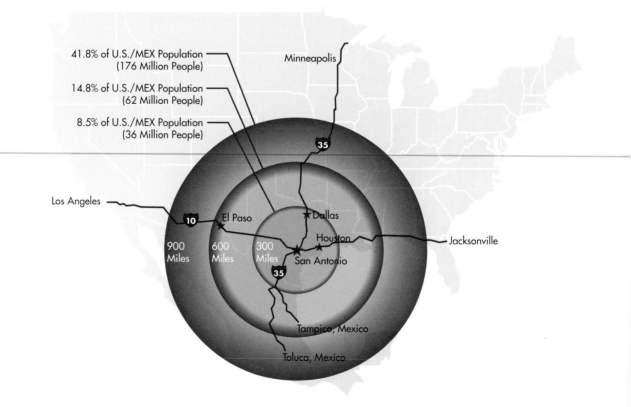

41.8% of U.S./MEX Population (176 Million People)

14.8% of U.S./MEX Population (62 Million People)

8.5% of U.S./MEX Population (36 Million People)

Minneapolis

Los Angeles

El Paso

Dallas

Houston

Jacksonville

San Antonio

900 Miles

600 Miles

300 Miles

Tampico, Mexico

Toluca, Mexico

Texas Has the Most Freight Infrastructure in the United States

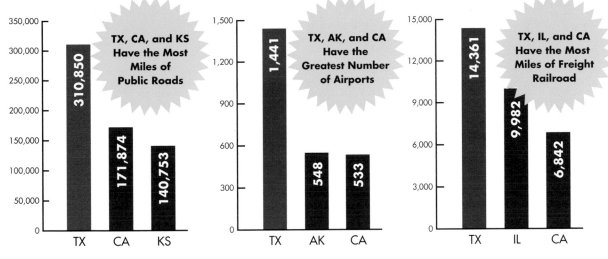

TX, CA, and KS Have the Most Miles of Public Roads

- TX: 310,850
- CA: 171,874
- KS: 140,753

TX, AK, and CA Have the Greatest Number of Airports

- TX: 1,441
- AK: 548
- CA: 533

TX, IL, and CA Have the Most Miles of Freight Railroad

- TX: 14,361
- IL: 9,982
- CA: 6,842

Top 5 Imports and Exports That Cross the Border Through Texas

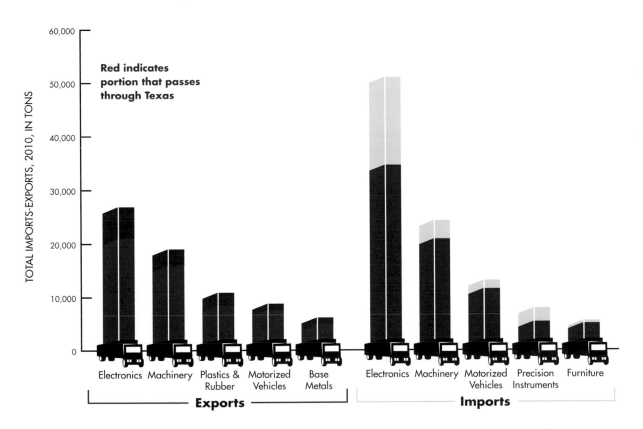

Red indicates portion that passes through Texas

TOTAL IMPORTS-EXPORTS, 2010, IN TONS

Exports: Electronics, Machinery, Plastics & Rubber, Motorized Vehicles, Base Metals

Imports: Electronics, Machinery, Motorized Vehicles, Precision Instruments, Furniture

THE WORLD'S PORT OF CALL

Texas Ports

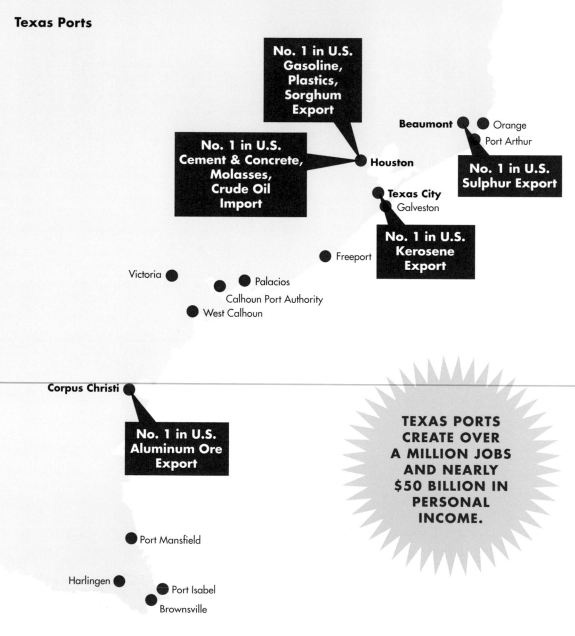

No. 1 in U.S.
Gasoline,
Plastics,
Sorghum
Export

No. 1 in U.S.
Cement & Concrete,
Molasses,
Crude Oil
Import

Beaumont — Orange
Port Arthur

Houston

No. 1 in U.S.
Sulphur Export

Texas City
Galveston

No. 1 in U.S.
Kerosene
Export

Freeport

Victoria
Palacios
Calhoun Port Authority
West Calhoun

Corpus Christi

No. 1 in U.S.
Aluminum Ore
Export

TEXAS PORTS
CREATE OVER
A MILLION JOBS
AND NEARLY
$50 BILLION IN
PERSONAL
INCOME.

Port Mansfield

Harlingen
Port Isabel
Brownsville

A half-billion tons of goods—a fifth of what America sells and buys abroad—enter or leave the country from Texas ports. The Lone Star State has four of the ten largest ports in the U.S., and Texas is the import and export leader in more than twenty different categories of goods, everything from gasoline to sorghum. Our biggest seafaring center, the Port of Houston, has been the top entry point for foreign goods for two decades. Houston alone traffics a greater tonnage of petroleum, iron, and steel than the Panama Canal, and it is a primary point of entry and exit for all sorts of other raw and refined materials, from animal fats to organic chemicals to cereal grains. With increased efforts to improve deep-draft construction and to improve inland intermodal transportation connections, the ports of Texas are sure to stay on top.

Texas Share of Total U.S. Shipping Exports

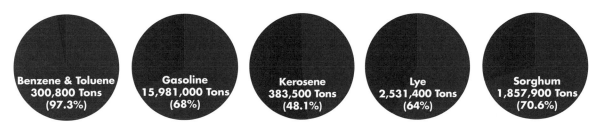

Benzene & Toluene 300,800 Tons (97.3%)

Gasoline 15,981,000 Tons (68%)

Kerosene 383,500 Tons (48.1%)

Lye 2,531,400 Tons (64%)

Sorghum 1,857,900 Tons (70.6%)

Texas vs. the Panama Canal

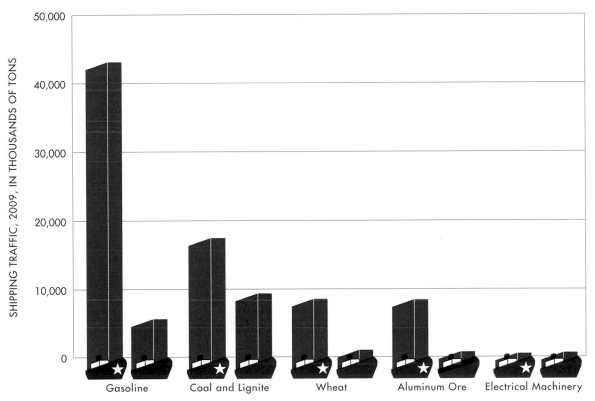

SHIPPING TRAFFIC, 2009, IN THOUSANDS OF TONS

Gasoline   Coal and Lignite   Wheat   Aluminum Ore   Electrical Machinery

TEXAS IS STILL
COWBOY COUNTRY

"Oh, a ten-dollar hoss and a forty-dollar saddle,
And I'm goin' to punchin' Texas cattle…"
— *Traditional song, author unknown*

Texas is the cattle capital of America. It leads the country in beef production, and more than 11 million head of cattle call the state home. Today, ranching constitutes the largest portion of Texas's agricultural sector by an

order of magnitude. And while the era of the great trail drives (see page 50) may be over, the traditions of cowboy life, from rodeos to livestock auctions, are alive and well all across the Lone Star State.

This page: A 1930s rancher looks over his cattle stock.
Opposite: In February 2012, eighteen-year-old Cuatro Schauer from Beeville, Texas, sold Spider Monkey, a 1,328-pound European Cross steer, for $230,000 at the Fort Worth Stock Show.

TEXAS HAS ABOUT TWICE AS MANY COWS AS NEBRASKA, ITS CLOSEST BEEF COMPETITOR.

TEXAS GAME-CHANGER
SAMUEL MAVERICK

mav·er·ick

*1: an unbranded range animal;
especially: a motherless calf
2: an independent individual who does
not go along with a group or party*

— *Merriam Webster's Dictionary*

The first thing you've gotta know about the word *maverick* is that it's got only two syllables: MAV-rick. The second thing is that the word comes from a Texan, Samuel Augustus Maverick. A land baron, businessman, scrappy independence fighter, and canny politician, Sam Maverick fit the definition of the word coined from his family name.

Maverick was born in the backcountry of South Carolina in 1803, went to college at Yale, studied law in Virginia, and passed the bar back home in South Carolina. After shooting a supporter of the senator and legendary orator John C. Calhoun (who happened to be Maverick's neighbor) in a duel and nursing his foe back to health in his home, Maverick migrated to northern Alabama with his sister to manage one of his father's plantations.

On trips to New York and New Orleans, Maverick heard talk about Texas, and he soon knew in his heart that his future was not on the Alabama plantation but in the hoped-for Lone Star Nation. Upon hearing of his son's plans to go to Texas, the elder Maverick advised him to buy as much land as he could. Maverick followed his father's advice and would go on to become one of the largest landowners in the territory.

He arrived in Velasco in 1835, on the eve of the revolution against Mexican rule, and was one of the Texas rebels. In 1836, he was elected to represent San Antonio at the signing of the Texas Declaration of Independence and narrowly missed being killed at the Alamo because he was on his way to Washington-on-the-Brazos for the gathering.

In 1842, after Texas had become an independent nation, Maverick, along with fifty-five other Texans, was captured by Mexican troops and led on a forced march to a Veracruz prison. From South Carolina, Maverick's father negotiated with the Mexican government for his son's release, which the Mexicans made conditional on Maverick's swearing an oath of allegiance to the Mexican re-annexation of Texas. Maverick refused. Then, with no explanation, the Mexicans released him and two other prisoners in March 1843. Maverick returned to San Antonio triumphant, carrying his prison shackles as a souvenir. By the time of his death in 1870, Maverick had become the model of a true Texan: loyal to the people he was elected to serve, and loyal to Texas, his own promised land, a place he deemed worth fighting and dying for. Maverick was also a consummate entrepreneur; he owned a bank, a hotel, and a printing company.

In 1845, Samuel Augustus reluctantly accepted 400 Longhorn cattle in settlement of a debt. He refused to brand the herd and let it run free on his 385,000-acre spread on Matagorda Island. Some say it was an ingenious plan to claim all unbranded cattle as his own. Whatever the case, it soon came to pass that whenever a cowboy stumbled across one of Sam's unbranded animals or their many off-spring, they'd say, "That's a maverick." By the end of

the Civil War and the chaos it brought, the Texas range was filled with unbranded animals that had grown into big bulls with large horns. The state of Texas soon passed a law that said all brands had to be registered in their county of origin and subsequently declared all animals with unregistered brands "mavericks." It was only toward the end of the century that *maverick* came to take on the meaning most frequently ascribed to it today.

Opposite: Samuel Maverick, undated. This page, below left: Maverick built his two-story house on the Alamo Plaza in honor of all that had transpired there. In an 1847 letter to his wife, Mary, he wrote, "I have a desire to reside on this particular spot, a foolish prejudice, no doubt, as I was almost a solitary escape from the Alamo massacre having been sent by those unfortunate men [to the independence convention]." From the second floor, Sam and Mary would likely have had a view of the mission. Below right: A handwritten page from Maverick's journal dated March 16, 1835.

MAVERICK'S GRANDSON, U.S. CONGRESSMAN MAURY MAVERICK, COINED THE TERM *GOBBLEDYGOOK*.

THE NEW GREAT MIGRATION
LEADS HERE

Above: The lights from downtown Dallas reflect in the Trinity River. Opposite: Because of the diversity of jobs available, "this is the best place in the country to live," said Irving City Councilman Dennis Webb in a recent Governing.com article.

The 2010 Census proved that Texas is one of the top destinations for the growing wave of African-Americans who are leaving the North and the Left Coast behind. This shift is a dramatic reversal of the decades-long Great Migration of the 20th century, which brought millions of blacks from the South to northern industrial hubs like Chicago, Detroit, and New York, as well as to Los Angeles and San Francisco. Today, African-Americans have decided that opportunity lies not in the old urban enclaves of the North but in diverse, dynamic, job-generating cities like Houston and Dallas, which was ranked number two nationally in black population growth from 2000 to 2010 and was ranked number five in *Black Enterprise* magazine's list of the ten best cities for African-Americans. As for Houston, it was ranked by BET.com as the best city in the entire country for African-American families to live in. Not only are black newcomers to Texas cities young and well-educated—creating a significant "brain gain" in the state—but they are moving to racially diverse suburbs instead of inner-city neighborhoods. Twenty percent of the growth in the African-American population in the last decade took place in counties that had been home to only a tiny number of black people. While historical and kinship ties have played a part in this reverse migration, many African-Americans see in Texas the makings of a life in which community is centered not around race but around the universal values of prosperity and opportunity.

A POPULATION MAGNET

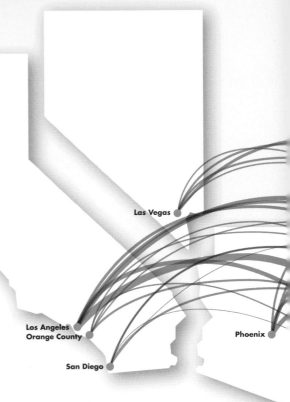

"Between 2004 and 2007, more people left California for Texas and Oklahoma than came to California in the Dust Bowl era."

—David Kennedy, Pulitzer Prize–winning author, in his remarks at the Aspen Ideas Festival, 2012

Welcome to the new land of milk and honey. Onetime migration hubs like Southern California, Phoenix, and Las Vegas are losing out to Texas's booming urban counties in terms of net inbound migration; so are traditional manufacturing centers like Chicago and Detroit. Even Brooklyn is bleeding population to Texas. And that's just half the story. It's not just how many newcomers these Texas cities are getting, but what kind. Namely, high earners. Consider the migration numbers between Los Angeles and Travis County, Texas. Yes, five hundred or so Travis County residents packed up for Southern California in 2011, but their average income was just $25,700. Compare that with the 850 people who fled Greater L.A. for Travis County; their average income: $47,000. All told, Los Angeles lost a staggering $76 million in earning potential that year to the five Texas urban areas shown on the map at right. Chicago lost almost $44 million; Detroit, $14 million. That's a lot of talent and capital on the move.

Net Migration, Fiscal Year 2011

Into Texas

Out of Texas

>900 People	
800–900 People	
700–800 People	
600–700 People	
500–600 People	
400–500 People	
300–400 People	
200–300 People	
100–200 People	
0–100 People	

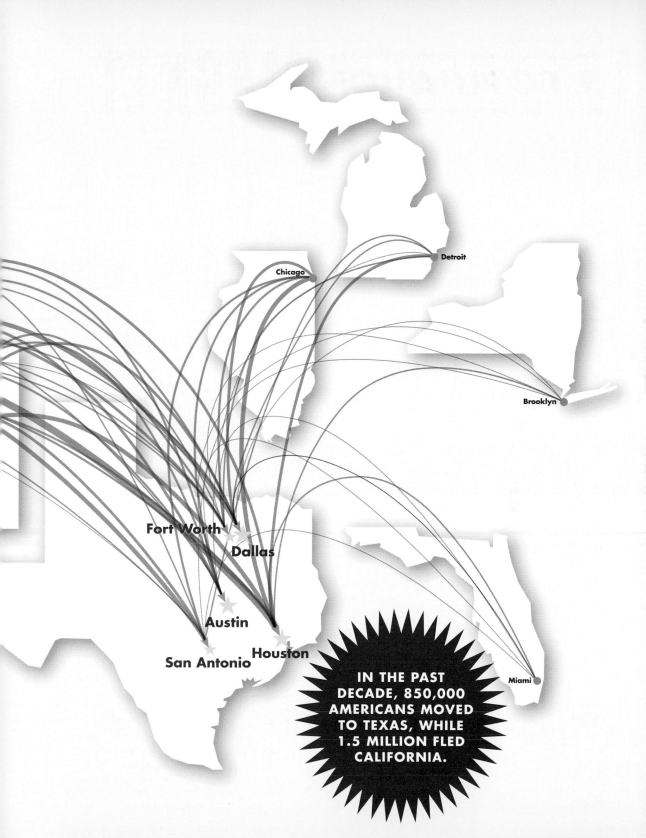

Chicago

Detroit

Brooklyn

Fort Worth

Dallas

Miami

Austin

Houston

San Antonio

IN THE PAST
DECADE, 850,000
AMERICANS MOVED
TO TEXAS, WHILE
1.5 MILLION FLED
CALIFORNIA.

POWERHOUSE METROS

Texas is home to twelve of the thirteen fastest-growing cities in the country, and its four biggest metropolitan areas—Dallas, Houston, Austin, and San Antonio—account for nearly three-quarters of the state's total GDP. Smaller metros account for much of the rest. The Lone Star State's cities are also job engines, contributing greatly to statewide employment. Sixteen Texas cities have regained 100 percent or more of the jobs lost during the Great Recession. Burgeoning urban centers like Austin, which has grown by some half-million people since 2000, are among the few markets in the country where home building is thriving. With their development-friendly policies and regulations, educated and affluent populations, and diverse local economies, the cities of Texas are primed to keep growing.

Rate of Population Growth, 2000–2010
Selected Metro Areas

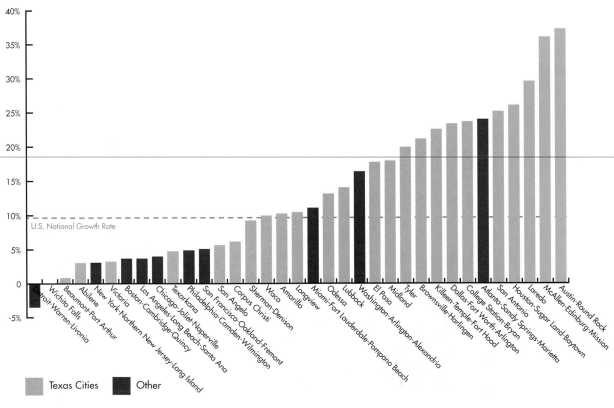

U.S. National Growth Rate

Texas Cities   Other

Texan Cities Add the Most Jobs in the Country

Job Growth, July 2008–February 2012

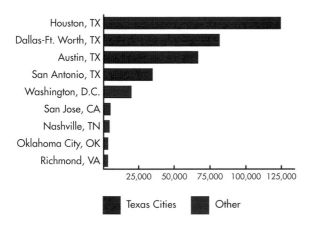

Houston, TX	
Dallas-Ft. Worth, TX	
Austin, TX	
San Antonio, TX	
Washington, D.C.	
San Jose, CA	
Nashville, TN	
Oklahoma City, OK	
Richmond, VA	

25,000 50,000 75,000 100,000 125,000

■ Texas Cities   ■ Other

Texas: Young at Heart

Texan cities have a younger median age than their counterparts across the United States, making them more dynamic and better positioned for years of economic growth.

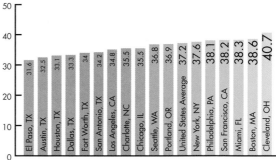

City	Median Age
El Paso, TX	31.6
Austin, TX	32.5
Houston, TX	33.1
Dallas, TX	33.3
Fort Worth, TX	34
San Antonio, TX	34.2
Los Angeles, CA	34.8
Charlotte, NC	35.5
Chicago, IL	35.5
Seattle, WA	36.8
Portland, OR	36.9
United States Average	37.2
New York, NY	37.6
Philadelphia, PA	38.1
San Francisco, CA	38.2
Miami, FL	38.3
Boston, MA	38.6
Cleveland, OH	40.7

Cost of Doing Business in Texas Metros (and Other Metros) Relative to the U.S. National Average

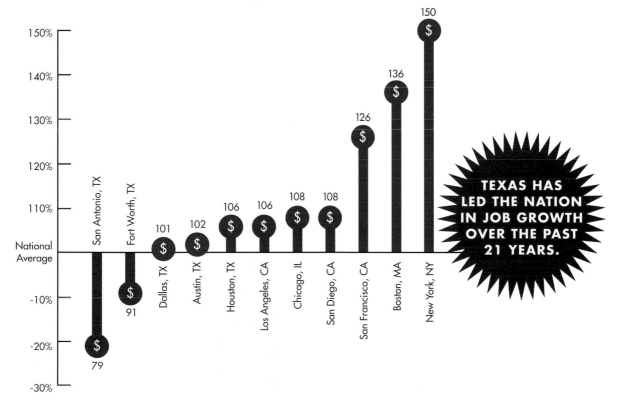

TEXAS HAS LED THE NATION IN JOB GROWTH OVER THE PAST 21 YEARS.

OUR POLITICIANS PUT PEOPLE
BEFORE PARTY

It's not a coincidence that two of the most success-ful independent presidential candidates in U.S. history hail from Texas. Ron Paul and Ross Perot are carrying on a populist tradition that dates to the days of Texas Governor Jim Hogg, the great 19th-century champion of the common man who made a political career of fighting monopoly power. The Lone Star State is very good at producing contrarian public figures who don't have much use for main-stream national political affiliations. Perhaps that's because Texas is also very good at producing self-made individuals who have done quite well for themselves by going it alone.

Ronald Ernest Paul worked for years as an obste-trician. He delivered more than four thousand babies. He's had an equally prolific career as an independent writer and publisher, having authored nine books that lay out his libertarian political and economic philosophy. Today he leads one of the most loyal, politically engaged—and youthful—followings of any candidate for national public office.

Henry Ross Perot, the son of a Texarkana mule trader and cotton buyer and a former IBM computer salesman, was already one of Texas's most successful entrepreneurs when he entered politics. In 1968 *Fortune* magazine called him "the fastest, richest

RON PAUL
Libertarian for President

IN 2011, RON PAUL'S CAMPAIGN RECEIVED 63% OF ALL DONATIONS FROM MILITARY MEMBERS.

Ron Paul
Libertarian
for
President

VOTER ROUND UP
POSSE PEROT
DEPUTY

For the People
PEROT
By the People
© 1992
PRESIDENT OF THE UNITED STATES
WESTERN NEW YORK COMMITTEE TO DRAFT ROSS PEROT

Texan ever." In 1979 Perot put together the daring rescue of two of his company's employees from one of the Ayatollah Khomeini's prisons in Iran. In 1992—running against a Texan (George Bush I) and a quasi-Texan (Bill Clinton, who grew up just thirty miles east of Perot's Texarkana home)—he became the most successful third-party presidential candidate since Theodore Roosevelt. Perot got almost 20 percent of the vote. By injecting their energy and entrepreneurial drive into the presidential contest, Paul and Perot have fundamentally changed the political conversation in America.

Opposite: Ross Perot, rallying the Boston faithful on October 1, 1996, roughly a month before the presidential election. This page, top: Ron Paul supporters at a campaign rally. Above: A flyer from Paul's 1988 presidential campaign—his first of three bids for the White House.

ODDFELLOWS AND ICONOCLASTS
WELCOME

Texas has a long history of guiding men and women to their true calling. The early-Texas land baron, publisher, and legislator Jacob DeCordova was born in Jamaica, but it was in the fledgling Texas Republic that he found his life's purpose. Before he even arrived in this no-man's-land he was shipping supplies from New Orleans to aid the Texan rebels, in whose cause he saw the noblest human aspirations. Then, after their victory at San Jacinto in 1836, he established a lodge of the Oddfellows Society—a venerable mutual-aid organization—in the newly created Republic of Texas, the first Oddfellows chapter outside of U.S. borders. He saw in the great unpeopled expanses of Texas a collective destiny, and he hungered to explore, to chart out, and ultimately to populate those vast lands. In 1849 DeCordova, compiling the records and notes from his travels all over Texas in the years prior, copublished a map of the region that became the cartographic standard in Texas. That same year he and two other men founded and laid out lots for the town of Waco. DeCordova also bought land, lots of it, and began selling it off to settlers. When the Civil War cut off the flow of payments from his tenants, he refused to evict them. In later years he published guidebooks to Texas for both migrants and travelers, and he lectured on his adoptive homeland in the big cities of the east and in England. DeCordova was a one-man chamber of commerce and a true believer—a breed Texans came to know and love well.

A few decades after DeCordova platted out Waco, Texas, that town became home to another legendary true believer, William Cowper Brann—known as Brann the Iconoclast. That moniker came from the name of the highly opinionated magazine that Brann published out of Waco in the final years of his life, which was cut short in 1898 by the bullet of an aggrieved father, whose daughter was a Baylor student. (Brann managed to squeeze off a shot himself as he lay wounded, killing his assailant.) That Baptist university was one of the favored targets of *The Iconoclast*'s florid and scathing editorials, as were Episcopalians, East Coast aristocracy, and virtually anyone Brann deemed holier-than-thou. Of the Baptists, Brann once said, "I have nothing against [them]. I just believe that they were not held under long enough." It was yellow journalism at its yellowest, but reading Brann's columns today is fine entertainment. In *The Iconoclast*'s pages, Baylor is "a great storm center of misinformation" attended by "magdalenes" (i.e., women of ill repute). The guests at a New York society maven's party are "sartorial kings and pseudo-queens" who come and go like "a breath blown from the festering lips of half-forgotten harlots." In the wide-open spaces of Texas, Brann filled the air with words, and people drank them in. At the time of his death, *The Iconoclast*'s circulation had reached 100,000. Brann's gravestone, in Waco's Oakwood Cemetery, bears no name or dates. Just the word *TRUTH*—and two bullet holes.

Opposite, left: Jamaican by birth, Texan by nature, Jacob DeCordova was a noted landowner, lecturer, legislator, and publisher. Opposite, right: Treating his desk as a soapbox, William Cowper Brann stuck it to holier-than-thou foes, penning scathing editorials for his magazine, *The Iconoclast*. This page, below: Compiled from DeCordova's landmark topographic surveys, this hand-drawn 1856 map includes counties, cities, roads, railways, and topographical information.

DECORDOVA'S TEXAS, HER RESOURCES AND HER PUBLIC MEN (1858) WAS THE FIRST-EVER ENCYCLOPEDIA OF THE STATE.

What happened at the Spindletop oil field in East Texas on January 10, 1901, is common knowledge in the Lone Star State. Indeed, the Lucas well gusher (right), which lasted for nine days and was the biggest oil strike anyone in the country had ever seen, has attained an almost mythic aura over the years. The same goes for what happened after: the mad rush to drill; the transformation of Beaumont, Texas, into the country's first oil boomtown; the birth, virtually overnight, of the petroleum industry. But the real lessons of this oft-told Texas tale are to be found in what happened before the gusher blew. Four tries had been made on Spindletop before Anthony Lucas's long-shot bet paid off. The Croatian-born prospector had

WE'VE GOT THE SPIRIT

OF A WILDCATTER

run out of money multiple times, got bogged down in the oil sands again and again, replaced one drill bit after another, and for months at a time endured the grim realities of daily life atop a barren, sun-baked salt dome that geologists of the day deemed worthless. In his relentless determination to wring something good from a nasty patch of earth, even in the face of failure, Lucas embodied to his very fiber the wildcatter's never-say-die spirit.

TEXAS LEADS THE NATION IN OIL PRODUCTION, CHURNING OUT SOME 52 MILLION BARRELS PER MONTH.

Detected 1,300 feet below the surface, the Spindletop gusher was, as of January 1901, the largest of its kind in the world.

..PLUS THE GRIT AND

GUTS OF A ROUGHNECK

Finding oil in Texas is no picnic. But getting it out of the ground is even tougher—just ask a roughneck. Of all the Texas tough-guy archetypes, the drill-rig worker is right up there with the cowboy and the Texas Ranger, and for good reason. A roughneck's job is the very definition of dirty work—you'll know why if you spend twelve hours a day sending steel pipe into a well bore and sucking the mud back out while staying out of the way of whipsawing spinner chains. And yet, for lots of Texans, working fourteen-day

springboard to the American dream. A high school grad can earn as much as $400 a day on a rig, and, with all his meals and lodging paid for, can sock almost all of it away. There are more than 900 rotary rigs (the most common kind) operating in Texas today—that's nearly half of all the working rigs in the country—and 38 percent of the nation's oil and gas extraction workers are employed in Texas.

In oil industry lingo, this type of well head is casually referred to as a Christmas tree—that's how they grow 'em in West

FOR OUR MONEY
THERE'S NO PLACE LIKE HOME

Between the Civil War and World War I, cotton, cattle, and oil were seeding newfound fortunes all over Texas, and entrepreneurs needed local institutions to bankroll their ventures. It took prudent risk-takers to get local banking off the ground in the state. Among them was one Thomas Claiborne Frost: lawyer, merchant, Latin teacher, Texas Ranger, Confederate Army colonel, and, finally, banker. The bank that bears his name today had its roots in the plight of cotton growers and wool makers, whose warehoused goods Frost used as collateral to make loans to these producers and growers—who in turn started depositing money with Frost.

Frost Bank soon became the quintessential hometown institution catering to local business interests. In more recent years, it became the only one of the ten biggest Texas banks to survive the 1979 oil-price crash and the savings-and-loan crisis of the 1980s and early '90s, when six hundred Texas banks and 90 percent of the state's S&Ls went bust. Thanks in part to reforms passed after the S&L mess, Texas largely avoided the subprime-loan crisis that triggered the

Great Recession. Today, banks like Frost have an ardent fan in Richard Fisher, the head of the Dallas Fed (see page 166). Foreseeing a repeat of the S&L calamity, Fisher has called for the bust-up of New York City's "too big to fail" banks. He frequently points to Texas banks as examples of a healthy, regionally driven financial sector. As well he should: According to the FDIC, Texas banks in 2011 were five times as profitable as U.S. banks overall and were charging off bad loans at less than half the rate of banks nationwide.

IN 2009, AS THE NATION'S BANKING INDUSTRY LOST $11.5 BILLION, TEXAS BANKS EARNED $1.4 BILLION.

Left: When Frost, a former mercantile trader, launched his banking business, it was among the first of its kind in San Antonio. Above: As Texas banking has grown, so too has its architecture. The simple storefronts of yore have given way to skyscrapers like the Frost Bank Tower, the third-tallest building in Austin, dedicated in 2004.

TEXAS GAME-CHANGER
SID RICHARDSON

Self-made men with big personalities and big wallets are what you might call a renewable resource in Texas, a state with a history of breeding swashbucklers who know how to turn pure grit into piles of money. But Texas has never known anyone quite like Sid Richardson. This eccentric and famously generous Fort Worth oil and cattleman somehow managed both to fit the type and to defy it.

Born in 1891 to an Athens, Texas, saloon owner, Richardson straddled two eras, coming of age just as cotton and cows were giving way to crude as the favored means of getting rich in the Lone Star State. He got his start trading in cattle and made big money trading in oil. Richardson's road to riches was neither short nor straight, however. His world-view would forever be tempered by his bumpy ride during the early boom-and-glut years of the Texas oil industry, during which he made and lost a fortune several times over. It wasn't until he struck it big with the Keystone Field in West Texas in 1935 that Richardson found himself poised to enter the fraternity of the Big Rich.

Richardson was a consummate opportunist. During the Depression, he was able to see opportunity where others saw obstacles. When the state of Texas and other oil-producing states started enforcing stricter production limits to stabilize oil prices in the early 1930s, Richardson read the winds and realized that stability would work in his favor. "[W]ith regulated production and stable prices, banks and other lenders began to look more favorably on settled production as security for loans," write Roger M. Olien and Diana Davids Hinton in their book *Wildcatters: Texas Independent Oilmen*. Soon, Richardson got loans from the First National Bank of Dallas and from banks in New York, Chicago, and Boston. He also attracted private investors in his oil partnerships, like the prominent publisher Charles E. Marsh.

By the 1940s Richardson had transformed from oil man to oil baron. With returns flowing in from

the Keystone Field and other West Texas wells, he moved himself out of his old storefront offices in Fort Worth and started leasing oil tracts, running cattle ranches, and acquiring a diverse portfolio of assets, including a broadcasting network, a carbon black plant, and a refining company. According to Bryan Burrough, author of *The Big Rich: The Rise and Fall of the Greatest Texas Oil Fortunes*, Richardson at one time "controlled more petroleum reserves than three major oil companies." Soon he'd joined the ranks of contemporaries Clint Murchison, H. L. Hunt, and Hugh Roy Cullen, oil men whose fortunes had been forged during the Depression and who had emerged in the 1940s and '50s as some of the richest and most powerful men in Texas. Many came to know them as the Big Four.

Of this group, Sid Richardson was probably the most private and the most plainspoken. "Luck helped me every day of my life," he once said. "And I'd rather be lucky than smart, 'cause a lot of smart people ain't eatin' regular." His knack for distilling the complexities of business into nuggets of homespun wisdom, combined with his wealth, brought governors, senators, and presidents to his doorstep.

Richardson made big contributions to Lyndon Johnson's 1948 campaign for the Senate, and in 1951 he became a prime supporter of Dwight Eisenhower's bid for the presidency. Ike promised Texas that she could keep her "tideland royalties" in the Gulf of Mexico. This oil and gas revenue has helped pay for college educations for millions of Texans in the sixty years since.

Richardson died in 1959, and his legacy is enduring. A bachelor, he left $50 million to the four sons of his nephew, Perry Bass; their collective inheritance is now at least a hundred times that amount. Today, no fewer than a dozen institutions—including a major charity and a museum showcasing Richardson's Western-art collection—bear the name of this former Athens, Texas, saloon keeper's son.

PRESIDENT EISENHOWER WAS BORN IN DENISON, TEXAS, AND PROPOSED TO HIS WIFE, MAMIE, IN SAN ANTONIO.

Opposite: Richardson (left) gives a big Texas welcome to President Eisenhower, whom he had urged to run for office. This page, left: Derricks dot the landscape of the Spindletop oil field, circa 1930. Right, clockwise from top left: Perry Bass and sons Sid, Robert, and Edward.

BETWEEN A ROCK AND A HARD PLACE
★ *WE THRIVE* ★

At some point every young industry hits a brick wall—some physical or technological barrier that requires a quantum leap in innovation. In 1907 the fledgling Texas oil industry hit something harder: bedrock. That was the year that drilling contractors Walter B. Sharp and Howard R. Hughes came up against an impenetrable layer of rock at their Goose Creek well. This was hardly a new problem for oil prospectors, and Hughes was determined to solve it. He retreated for two weeks to his parents' home in Iowa to rethink the very DNA of the drill bit, which until that point was basically a pointy thing that chipped and scraped away at rock—a method that worked fine for clay and soft stone, but not hard bedrock. Hughes's breakthrough? He figured out how to create a single bit with multiple interlocking cones. Its tough steel teeth could grind and pulverize even the hardest limestone. The Hughes Rock Bit, when it was finally patented and widely put to use in 1909, penetrated hard rock at ten times the speed of any other bit out there. The Hughes Tool Company ultimately made twenty-odd patented improvements to that drill bit in the years that followed, and they became the seed for the fortune Hughes's famous aviator son would inherit.

Around 1950, a facsimile of a drill bit, modeled after the Hughes Tool Company hard formation rock bit type R-1, was fashioned into this trophy.

BEFORE DRILLING FOR OIL, HUGHES STUDIED LAW AT HARVARD AND THE UNIVERSITY OF IOWA.

★ SMALL OIL IS STILL ★
GOING STRONG

There are roughly five thousand oil companies in Texas. A few of them, like ExxonMobil and Texaco, are huge multinationals, but hundreds of others are mom-and-pop operations comprising a few "stripper" wells that produce a comparative trickle. The history of oil in this state is also the history of how these independents have survived in the face of the oil giants. Their reigning symbol is the mechanical pumping jack, which we call the State Bird of Texas. If you've driven almost anywhere in the state, you've seen them, maybe whole fields of them, bobbing their heads on the horizon like those little drinking-bird toys. These machines are the real workhorses of the onshore oil industry in Texas. Sure, we love the notion of oil gushing from the ground of its own free will, but a lot of petroleum reservoirs don't generate that kind of pressure, at least not for long, which means drillers have to coax crude from the earth mechanically. The sight of those jacks rocking back and forth tirelessly under the Texas sky reminds us that in a land of wildcatters and entrepreneurs, you can't sit back and expect prosperity to flow forth like a geyser. You've got to work for it.

THE WORLD'S
DEEP-DRILLING PIONEER

The history of offshore oil and gas drilling in the Gulf of Mexico, and all around the world, is the story of men finding ever more ingenious ways of sending drills deep into the ocean floor. And it's largely been Texans who have written that story. They've produced most of the pioneering innovations in offshore and deepwater drilling, and those innovations have not only opened up vast new sources of energy, but all that new technology has also gone on to help humankind in other ways—

from mapping the ocean floor to saving lives on container ships caught in storms. Today, offshore drilling accounts for more than a quarter of the natural gas produced in the United States and more than 30 percent of our domestic oil production. While the first offshore rigs were able to drill only in 20 or so feet of water, today there are open-water rigs out there that can send a drill almost 30,000 feet into the subocean crust while floating on open water 10,000 feet deep.

A Brief History of Offshore Tech

1933

The Texas Company (later Texaco) introduces a derrick mounted on a submersible barge. This new type of shallow-water rig can be set up in as little as a day, and quickly refloated and towed to a new location, enabling easy exploration of the oil-rich Texan wetlands.

1937

An East Texas construction company, Brown & Root, builds the first oil-producing well in open water in the Gulf of Mexico. Its 320-foot-tall wooden drilling deck a mile and a half offshore is the first freestanding structure in the ocean.

1947

Brown & Root builds a rig on wooden pilings in fifteen feet of water, ten miles out to sea in the Gulf of Mexico. It is the first offshore oil well out of sight of land.

1954

Houston's Humble Oil uses data from wave-measuring devices to dramatically improve the ability of large rigs and ships to survive storms on the open sea.

1955

A Corpus Christi engineer invents the "Billy Pugh Net," named after himself. The padded floating ring with an upright net reduces the number of accidents and fatalities involved in transferring rig workers from boats to the platform. This same technology will later be used to collect the Apollo astronauts after splashdown in the ocean.

1957

Divers working in the Gulf of Mexico pioneer the use of recompression chambers and mixed-gas tanks in order to service a new generation of deeper rigs. By the mid-1960s, the Houston-based Shell Oil Company will demonstrate the potential of helium-oxygen mixtures to bring divers down to depths of 1,000 feet.

Early 1960s

Shell begins development of a remotely operated vehicle that carries a TV camera, sonar, and a mechanical claw that allows it to tighten bolts, close valves, and attach hoses. Shell's prototypes will ultimately serve as the basis for the remotely operated submersibles that help discover the wreck of the *Titanic* in 1985.

1961

The *CUSS I* research vessel makes the first penetration of the hard rock of the earth's crust to underlying volcanic formations, drilling in almost 12,000 feet of water.

The Growing Impact of Deep-Drilling Technology

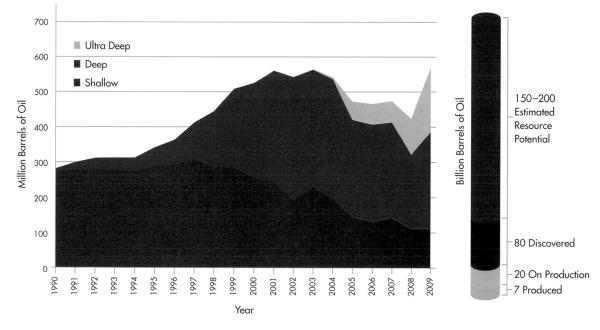

Million Barrels of Oil (y-axis)

Legend:
- Ultra Deep
- Deep
- Shallow

X-axis years: 1990, 1991, 1992, 1993, 1994, 1995, 1996, 1997, 1998, 1999, 2000, 2001, 2002, 2003, 2004, 2005, 2006, 2007, 2008, 2009

Year

The Future of Deep Drilling

Billion Barrels of Oil (y-axis)

- 150–200 Estimated Resource Potential
- 80 Discovered
- 20 On Production
- 7 Produced

1962
Shell introduces *Bluewater I,* a semi-submersible that can operate in hundreds of feet of ocean water without needing to rest on the bottom. Oil producers can now drill in waters too deep for anchoring.

1968
The Levingston Shipbuilding Company, in Orange, Texas, launches the *Glomar Challenger,* which becomes the first ship to drill in more than 20,000 feet of water, opening up the world's deep-ocean basins. The drilling samples it collects also provide definitive proof for the theory of plate tectonics.

1970s and 1980s
3-D seismic techniques, primarily developed by Dallas-based Geophysical Services Inc., quadruple the known amount of recoverable oil and gas in the Gulf.

1978
Oceaneering International of Houston debuts the Newtsuit, a hard-body diving suit equipped with thrusters that allows divers to work at depths of 1,000 feet for long periods of time without the need for decompression or complicated mixed-gas breathing. The technology soon migrates to other industries like salvage, photographic survey, and scientific deep-sea exploration.

Late 1970s to Early 1980s
Texas-based ExxonMobil pioneers the development of zero-discharge rigs, designed with closed-loop systems that allow nothing (not even rainwater runoff) to end up in the sea.

2012
Houston-based Marine Well Containment Company unveils a blowout containment system featuring a 100-ton "capping stack" that safely plugs wells in 10,000 feet of water and can divert 100,000 barrels of oil a day, contributing to the U.S. government's decision to begin reissuing permits for deepwater drilling in the Gulf.

TEXAS GAME-CHANGER
RICHARD KINDER

When Richard Kinder was working at Enron in the early 1990s, he was uneasy about the giddy, asset-light direction the company was taking under the leadership of his boss and old college buddy, Kenneth Lay. Kinder was hands-on, results-oriented, and very focused on natural gas; Lay liked networking and deal-making. In 1996, Kinder quit Enron and was replaced by the soon-to-be-infamous former McKinsey & Company consultant Jeff Skilling. It turned out that the "smartest guy in the room" was neither Skilling nor Lay but the guy who'd just quit Enron.

In a dynamic boom-and-bust city like Houston, where wheeling and dealing is a religion unto itself, it takes a certain self-possession to keep your feet on the ground. Kinder, a Vietnam vet and former real estate guy who'd been through bankruptcy himself in the early '80s, could see through the cigar smoke in Lay and Skilling's illusory world, where being worshiped by the best and brightest of Wall Street was considered the highest possible goal.

In his extraordinary post-Enron career, Kinder has stuck to pipelines and their steady cash flow. Kinder remained firm in his belief that pipelines were the perfect infrastructure assets—the profitable underground toll roads of the oil-and-gas industry. If there were enough gas or oil reserves at the entry point—and if you had the foresight to envision how new technologies like fracking and improved directional drilling would create a lot more of those reserves (see page 85)—you could be sure that fifteen to twenty years into the future, the asset would still

Major Oil and Gas Pipelines in Texas

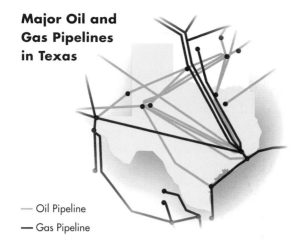

— Oil Pipeline

— Gas Pipeline

Opposite: Richard Kinder at the 2009 Reuters Energy Summit in Houston. This page, clockwise from left: Pipelines have always been a natural part of the Texas landscape; a tanker is docked at a Kinder Morgan facility in Los Angeles; pipe is stacked for use in the construction of a section of the Kinder Morgan, Inc., Rockies Express Natural Gas Pipeline outside of Laramie, Wyoming.

be pumping out a steady return. It's also highly unlikely that a competitor will lay a rival pipe next door. All of which means that owners can assure pension funds that their investment will pay out when their pension holders retire.

In 1997, Kinder and his college friend Bill Morgan raised partnership money to buy the Enron Liquids Pipeline that Ken Lay and Jeff Skilling wanted to cast off. Then they merged with KN Energy, a troubled natural-gas-pipeline company, and changed the new entity's name to Kinder Morgan, which quickly became a major player in the pipeline business. In late 2006, Kinder assembled a consortium of private-equity firms, and he and his senior managers took Kinder Morgan private for $15 billion. The deal was one of the largest private-equity transactions in history. In 2011, Kinder Morgan bought out the El Paso Corporation, a rival pipeline company, for $21 billion

to create the largest oil-and-gas transportation company in North America. Since its inception, Kinder Morgan Energy Partners has delivered a compound annual return of 27 percent to its partnership's unit holders.

Kinder's shrewd but bold corporate stewardship has made him a rich man—the richest in Houston in 2011, according to *Forbes*. And he is a Houstonian through and through. In 2010 the Kinder Foundation, established with his wife, Nancy, in the late '90s, awarded a $30 million grant to the city's parks system to improve the public spaces around Houston's bayous. They endowed an urban research institute at Rice University and have supported plenty of other worthy causes. For Kinder, it's all part of the same life mission. "In Houston," he once said, "you are what you achieve. That's my idea of the American dream."

AT&T Finances

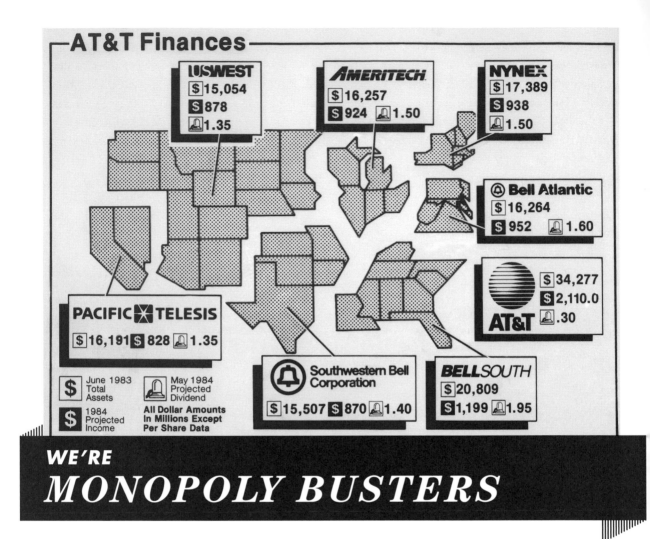

US WEST
- $ 15,054
- S 878
- 1.35

AMERITECH
- $ 16,257
- S 924
- 1.50

NYNEX
- $ 17,389
- S 938
- 1.50

Bell Atlantic
- $ 16,264
- S 952
- 1.60

AT&T
- $ 34,277
- S 2,110.0
- .30

PACIFIC TELESIS
- $ 16,191 S 828 1.35

Southwestern Bell Corporation
- $ 15,507 S 870 1.40

BELLSOUTH
- $ 20,809
- S 1,199 1.95

$	June 1983 Total Assets
S	1984 Projected Income
📖	May 1984 Projected Dividend
	All Dollar Amounts In Millions Except Per Share Data

WE'RE
MONOPOLY BUSTERS

Ding-dong! Ma Bell is dead! And it was Texans, including us Wylys, who helped bust up the AT&T monopoly and bring the giant down. You'd never know it today, with the Wyly Theater and the AT&T Performing Arts Center standing close by each other as happy Dallas neighbors, but back in the '60s and '70s, we were sworn enemies.

It was a long fight to get to January 1982, when Judge Harold H. Greene ordered AT&T to bust itself into seven pieces, thereby releasing its monopolistic grip—long sanctioned by the federal government—on the U.S. telephone market. The decision was the final blow in an eight-year antitrust battle with the Department of Justice.

Rewind to 1968, when the Federal Communications Commission allowed Dallas inventor Tom P. Carter to access the AT&T network without using Bell equipment. Carter had developed the Carterfone, a nifty device that linked two-way radio systems to telephone lines, enabling folks in the Texas oil fields to chat with people on landlines. It was basically the first cell phone, and it marked the beginning of the end for the telephone monopoly in the United States. Soon other countries would follow our lead.

The following year, Microwave Communications, Inc., or MCI, won permission from the FCC to sell private phone lines to businesses. Goliath was reeling, and the next Dallas-based David to pick up a slingshot was University Computing Company, a company I (Sam) started in 1963. Our tussle with AT&T had nothing to do with competing for voice customers; UCC sold computer services to corporations and, after 1966, was looking to find ways to get computers to talk to one another.

Ma Bell's antiquated analog lines couldn't send data fast enough, and since the huge company had no competition, they were agonizingly slow in giving us computer guys the speed, accuracy, and flexibility we needed. So I formed Datran, the first all-digital phone company for computers, and we set out to build a string of microwave towers, spaced twenty to thirty miles apart, all across the USA. We scouted land and secured the necessary permits, and we hired three hundred of the best and brightest telecommunications folks ever assembled, but Ma Bell wasn't about to let some pesky Texans invade her turf.

In a classic case of status quo versus innovation and government sloth versus entrepreneurial agility, Ma Bell—then the biggest company in the world—tried to thwart our efforts, arguing that there was no demand for our digital network. After we proved them wrong, they argued that they could meet the demand. In 1971 the FCC ruled in our favor, but the monopoly used its power to intimidate both Wall Street and Congress. They convinced the banks to cancel their commitments to Datran. We had to shut down in 1976.

We lost the battle but won the war. The impact of the victory can't be overstated. Ma Bell's breakup led directly to the birth of the Internet, the telecommunications revolution, and the creation of hundreds of thousands of thriving software and hardware companies, among them Facebook, Google, and Apple. Monopolies are bad for business, and in Texas, that means they're marked for death.

UNIVERSITY COMPUTING COMPANY'S 1965 IPO EARNED A 100-1 RETURN IN FIVE YEARS.

Opposite: In 1982, AT&T agreed to break itself up into seven entities. This page, left: Sam Wyly created the term "computer utility" to describe the marriage of the telephone and the computer, which today means the Internet—the happy union that would change the world. His red 1966 Mustang is parked outside. Right, from left: Sam, Walter Heffner, and Glenn Penisten in front of a microwave tower on Cedar Hill, near Dallas, in 1972.

THE COUNTRY'S
WIND-ENERGY
LEADER

Texas produces more wind energy than any other state by far, having outstripped California years ago. In 2008 we launched a $5 billion program to build new transmission lines to carry wind-generated electricity to Dallas and other big cities—the largest public investment in renewable energy in U.S. history. And Texas isn't just jumping on the wind-power bandwagon; in fact, you could say we built the wagon. Way back in 1970, before dwindling oil supplies and global warming were hot-button issues, West Texas State University was already starting research on wind energy. Then, in 1977, two years before the first serially produced modern wind turbines even became available, WTSU (now West Texas A&M) founded the Alternative Energy Institute, which has been a leader in renewable energy development ever since.

Even the most hard-eyed oil man will tell you that wind is good business. In 2008, Texas oil and gas magnate and hostile-takeover king T. Boone Pickens went before Congress and proposed a major energy-policy overhaul that included the extensive development of the wind corridor running from Texas through the Great Plains. "We're the Saudi Arabia of wind," Pickens said. He showed how a dramatic growth in job creation would result from wind-related infrastructure and energy-transmission projects. The Pickens Plan won the praise of such varied figures as Carl Pope, the head of the Sierra Club, and New York City mayor Michael Bloomberg. It's always nice to get support from afar, but really, we're just doing what we've always done in Texas: looking to our resources and making the most of them.

★ THE SHALE GAS REVOLUTION ★ STARTED HERE AND
IT'S FRACKIN' AMAZIN'!

People knew that North America's vast shale formations contained natural gas long before George Mitchell ordered his workers to start drilling the Barnett Shale in North Texas in the early 1980s. The question was how to get it out. At the time, no one believed you could extract natural gas from the highly nonporous rock, at least not without going broke. By figuring out new ways to use alternative drilling technologies, Mitchell proved everyone wrong. Using a combination of hydraulic fracturing and horizontal drilling, he discovered how to get gas out of that shale and still turn a profit. And so he did—to the tune of $3.5 billion, which is what

Oklahoma-based Devon Energy paid to buy Mitchell's company after the Barnett Shale breakthrough. Shale gas is a game-changer. Already a whopping 30 percent (and rising) of domestic natural-gas supplies come from shale. The new drilling technologies have extended the estimated life span of recoverable gas reserves in the U.S. to 118 years. There are potential, but manageable, environmental risks to shale gas extraction, and Texas is going to lead the world in doing the job right.

Left: *Time* magazine hailed shale in an April 2011 cover story about the energy crisis. Right: Mitchell has been named among *Foreign Policy* magazine's top 100 global thinkers.

REMAKING AMERICA'S
ENERGY LANDSCAPE

Thanks in large part to Texans (see previous page), the production of natural gas from North America's vast shale basins has grown fourteen-fold in the last decade and is projected to double again by 2035. It all started with the Barnett Shale basin in Texas, where rig teams and engineers first figured out how to use a combination of horizontal drilling and hydraulic fracturing to get the gas out of all that nonporous rock. Now other basins like the Marcellus Shale, in the

Northeast, have begun to yield up their colossal energy potential, profoundly changing America's energy outlook for decades to come. Dirty old coal plants are being shut down, not just in Texas but in the Rust Belt too. In 2009, largely thanks to shale exploration, U.S. natural-gas production surpassed Russia's output for the first time in history, and by 2021 America will become a net exporter of natural gas. Rest assured, we will never again go to war over oil in the Persian Gulf.

Recoverable Shale Gas in the United States (Basins)

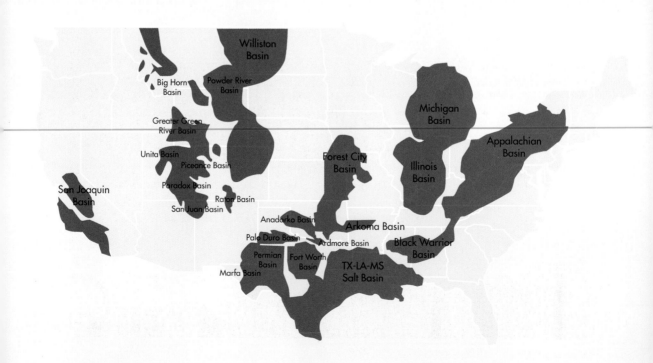

Production of Shale Gas in the United States, 2000 to 2011 (Fields)

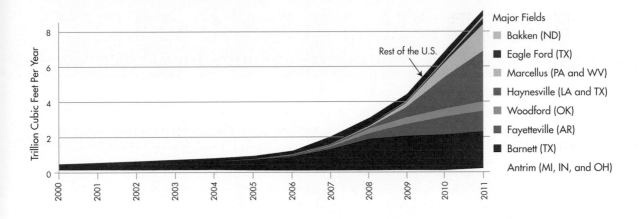

Trillion Cubic Feet Per Year

Rest of the U.S.

Major Fields
- Bakken (ND)
- Eagle Ford (TX)
- Marcellus (PA and WV)
- Haynesville (LA and TX)
- Woodford (OK)
- Fayetteville (AR)
- Barnett (TX)
- Antrim (MI, IN, and OH)

Production of Natural Gas in the United States, 1990 to 2035

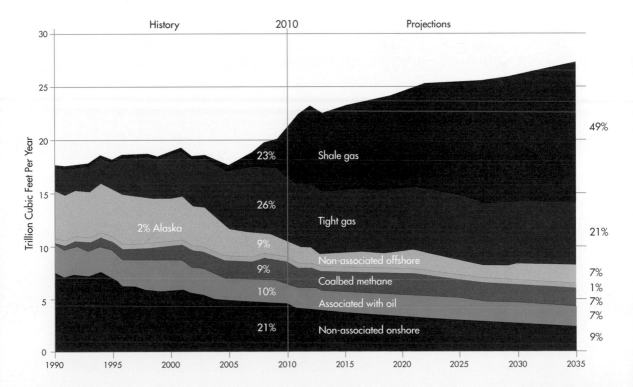

Trillion Cubic Feet Per Year

History   2010   Projections

2% Alaska

23% Shale gas   49%

26% Tight gas   21%

9%   Non-associated offshore   7%

9%   Coalbed methane   1%

10% Associated with oil   7%
                                        7%
21% Non-associated onshore   9%

WE DO DEREGULATION RIGHT

Texas is the only state in the union where consumers can really choose where they buy their electricity. Today 60 percent of the state's households buy their power from a private, competitive electricity provider, and 80 percent of Texas consumers favor a competitive electricity market. That's no surprise: They're paying less than they did before January 1, 2002, when Texas's landmark deregulation of the industry took effect, on time and on budget. But cost-per-kilowatt-hour is only part of the story. Deregulation opened the Texas market to renewable energy on a completely new scale, giving consumers their first real opportunity to buy sustainably generated power for their homes. Since 2002, the share of renewable energy—most of it from wind power (see page 84)—in Texas's electricity mix has gone from 1 percent to 7 percent, and it's growing steadily. What's more, the increased clean-energy supply, coupled with the Texas-led shale-gas revolution (see page 85), has handed a death sentence to coal power in Texas—no new coal plants will be built in the state ever again. And as clean energy use in Texas is rising, air pollution is plummeting. Levels of airborne nitrogen oxide dropped by a whopping 57.75 percent between 2000 and 2009. Noxious ground-level ozone levels dropped 27 percent over roughly the same period.

One of the reasons Texas knocked it out of the park with deregulation is that we had a good idea of how *not* to do it. In the late 1990s, as our state was gearing up for launching its competitive electricity market, a group of state lawmakers and regulators took a little trip to California to study how that state was handling its own electricity deregulation, begun in 1996. The answer was: not very well. "If this is what deregulation is," said one of those lawmakers, Steven Wolens, to a colleague, according to the *New York Times*, "we don't want it." His delegation saw an electricity regime in collapse. Prevented by environmental regulations from building new plants to feed increased demand, California was experiencing rolling blackouts. Electricity companies weren't allowed to enter into long-term contracts, making them vulnerable to price fluctuations. Even worse, companies had to buy their power on a centralized wholesale bidding market—controlled by the state! In sharp contrast, the Texas market has more than 175 providers of electricity and 247 retail plans.

President George W. Bush (pictured here with Ford CEO Alan Mulally at an alternative-fueled vehicles event in 2007), along with state representative Steve Wolens and state senator David Sibley, was paramount in establishing electricity deregulation in Texas.

...BUT WE'LL STILL STEP IN

TO HELP THE LITTLE GUY

As Texas proved in the early 2000s, deregulation is one way to bring down a giant—in that case a state-controlled electrical utility—and level the playing field for entrepreneurial competition. But history shows that we also know when to step in to protect the little guy against a goliath. Toward the end of the 19th century, the goliaths in Texas were the railroads, which, by the 1890s, controlled huge swaths of public land and were squeezing overland commerce in the grip of a monopoly. The railroads raised and lowered freight-carriage prices as they pleased, wreaking havoc on the livelihood of merchants, ranchers, and factory owners, who depended on rail transport to get their goods to market.

Enter James S. Hogg, who'd been elected governor of Texas in 1890. Hogg, an early standard bearer of the Progressive Era, said that he "knew the soul of the dirt farmer," and he blazed into office on a fiery platform of reform that promised to defend the common man against corporate forces. In 1891 he pushed through legislation that led to the formation of the Texas Railroad Commission, which successfully regulated passenger and freight prices and exposed wrongdoing on the part of the railroad operators.

The TRC eventually retooled itself for the oil era, helping to stabilize Texas's booming petroleum market during periods of uncontrolled growth and wildcatting. Today, writes David Prindle, the author of *Petroleum Politics and the Texas Railroad Commission*, the TRC consistently sides with independent producers and small landowners over major integrated companies. That's regulation, Texas style.

Travelers wait on the platform in Algoa, Texas, 1907.

TEXAS'S GREEN GRID

When it comes to delivering electricity, the map below says it all. You've got East, you've got West, and you've got Texas. We've got our very own power grid—power that's generated in Texas and delivered exclusively to Texans, creating a self-sufficient island that doesn't have to answer to federal regulators or schedule endless meetings with committees from other states. Texas is also the biggest producer of wind power in the nation (more than the next six states added together). Our independent grid, which encourages competitive bidding and reduces the obstacles to new infrastructure development, has facilitated an unprecedented public investment in renewable energy that other states haven't been able to achieve. In 2008 Texas approved a $5 billion plan to create new transmission lines to carry all that wind-generated electricity from West Texas (home to the two biggest wind farms in the world) to San Antonio, Fort Worth, and other major cities.

Major North American Electrical Grids

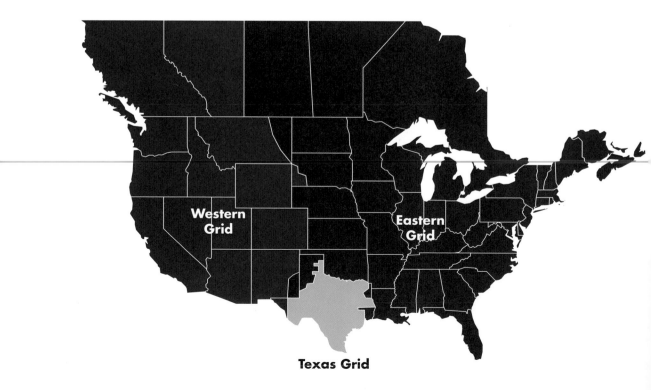

Western Grid

Eastern Grid

Texas Grid

Reduction in Texas Point Source NOx Emissions, A Main Precursor to Ozone Formation

Expenditure for New Transmission Lines in Texas Through 2017

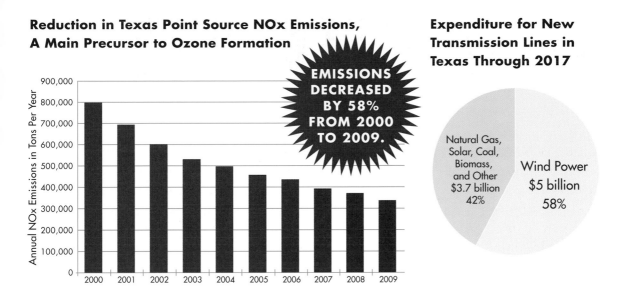

EMISSIONS DECREASED BY 58% FROM 2000 TO 2009.

Megawatts Generated by Wind in Top-Ten Wind-Power States

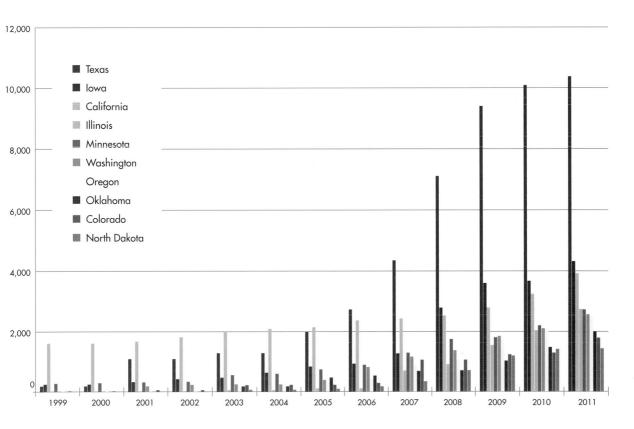

TEXAS GAME-CHANGER
GREEN MOUNTAIN ENERGY

In 2000, when the independent renewable-power company Green Mountain Energy moved to Texas—after banging its head against the wall in the overregulated environments of California, Ohio, and Pennsylvania—the idea of retail energy shopping, to say nothing of retail *clean*-energy shopping, was unknown to your average consumer. If things like solar and wind power were going to save the earth—so the thinking went—that kind of change was going to be dictated from above, not driven by free-market capitalism.

But the 2002 deregulation of Texas's power industry (see page 88) threw open the doors for people who wanted the option to buy electricity generated by cleaner sources. Green Mountain beat its competitors through that door, becoming the first clean-energy company to operate in Texas's competitive energy market. And it's had a major impact: Since 1997, Green Mountain customers have helped prevent more than 19.4 billion pounds of CO_2 emissions. Clearly, renewable energy is good business.

In Texas's newly fertile marketplace for private energy companies, Green Mountain saw the chance to get some big changes underway. "What we thought

THE CO$_2$
POLLUTION
GREEN MOUNTAIN
HAS PREVENTED
SINCE 1997
IS EQUIVALENT TO
RECYCLING
36 BILLION
CANS.

would happen has happened," said the company's senior vice president of marketing and strategic planning, Helen Brauner, in an interview with Greentech Media. "A lot more people understand now, and I think we had a hand in it, that electricity and pollution are connected."

Unfettered by state regulation, Green Mountain could dream big. In 2011 the company completed a two-year deal to be the exclusive provider of clean electricity to the Empire State Building, and in 2012 it partnered with the NFL to provide Super Bowl XLVI with 15 million kilowatt-hours of renewably sourced electricity. This is how sustainable energy gets on the map for average Americans. Today in Texas, clean energy is taking off, and older, coal-fired plants in Texas are being shut down.

"Part of what you're doing is voting for our energy future with every kilowatt-hour of electricity you use," said John Rogers, a senior energy analyst at the Union of Concerned Scientists, about Green Mountain Energy in *Grist* magazine in 2010. "[B]uying green power can make a real difference...."

Left: Green Mountain Energy donated four photovoltaic panels to the Museum of Nature & Science in Dallas. Above: The company also provides clean energy for the Empire State Building.

TEXAS GAME-CHANGER
CARRIE MARCUS NEIMAN

The idea of the department store wasn't born in Texas, but with the opening of the first Neiman Marcus emporium in Dallas in 1907, it was perfected here. Neiman Marcus remains today what it has been from the start: an artful combination of impeccable service, grandeur, and sheer good taste. For that we can thank a happy convergence of circumstances.

When Neiman Marcus opened, Dallas was a dusty frontier town of 78,000. The city and its outlying towns were home to hundreds of wealthy women—mostly the wives and daughters of cotton-, cattle-, and oilmen—and if those ladies wanted high fashion, they had to travel to New Orleans, New York, or even Europe in order to have dresses custom-tailored. *Quelle joie*, then, when they entered this ladies-wear wonderland, which offered the latest fashions, off the rack. Add to that a healthy dose of down-to-earth Texas cordiality, including a personal welcome when you walked in the store.

And finally, there was Carrie Marcus Neiman, the store's cofounder and guiding spirit. Seldom have mercantile savvy and a God-given sense of style so comfortably inhabited the same person. Born in Kentucky in 1883, Carrie Marcus was the youngest of five children of German immigrants and got to Dallas by way of Hillsboro, Texas. After high school, she worked in sales and married Abraham Lincoln "Al" Neiman, who ran a salvage business. There was a stint in Atlanta, where they worked briefly for a little-known soft-drink bottler called Coca-Cola. But Al deemed Coca-Cola a dead end, and so they returned to Dallas to start a retail store. With $25,000 in start-up money, Carrie, her husband, and her brother, Herbert, opened a fifty-foot store on Elm Street. They billed their establishment as "an exclusive shopping place for fashionable women" and sourced their inventory based wholly on Carrie Marcus Neiman's tastes. Theirs was the first specialty store for women's fashions in Texas.

The trio, all in their twenties, did not have a high school diploma among them, but they knew how to sell, Carrie especially. Their first printed advertisement said: "It shall be the store's policy to be a leader at all times." And yet Carrie's newfound role as Dallas's arbiter of fashion was never accompanied by haughtiness. Driving everything she did was an almost religious devotion to her customers. In 1913, a fire destroyed the original store along with every shred of merchandise. Fifteen bridal parties who'd recently placed orders with Neiman Marcus suddenly found themselves without gowns. By eleven o'clock that morning, Carrie had set up a makeshift workshop in a nearby hotel and started sewing dresses. All fifteen weddings went off without a hitch.

A year later, Neiman Marcus reopened in a four-story building at the corner of Main and Ervay, where the flagship store stands today. Acknowledging that Texas frontier women often needed fashion tutoring, Carrie and her partners saw the store as a sort of fashion finishing school, with shows and in-store events. They also expanded their offerings, now billing the establishment as "the store that can get you anything." Carrie and her partners tracked down the finest furs, antiques, jewelry, and exotica from all over the world.

In 1928 Carrie divorced Al Neiman, and her brother, Herbert, bought out Al's stock. Carrie continued her mission to put Dallas on the fashion map by sponsoring couture galas and expositions that drew models and designers from around the world. Today, Neiman Marcus is one of the last of the great luxury department stores that continues to operate under its original name and is still based in the city where it got its start.

One of Carrie's savviest innovations was the tradition—begun in 1952—of including in the store's annual Christmas catalog a handful of extravagant, aspirational gifts. The first such offering was a his-and-hers pairing: a live Black Angus steer for him and a solid silver roast-beef carving cart for her. Later editions of the Christmas Book included such whimsies as his-and-hers parasails ($316 each), his-and-hers hot-air balloons ($6,850), his-and-hers private airplanes ($176,000), and a $250,000 bag of uncut diamonds. The message was simple: To shop is to dream. And in Texas if you're going to dream, you might as well dream big.

Opposite: Carrie Marcus Neiman. This page, left, from left to right: Stanley Marcus, Lady Pamela Hicks with her father, the Earl Louis Mountbatten of Burma, and Mrs. Edward Marshall Boem at the Neiman Marcus British Fortnight Gala, 1973. Right: His-and-her camels are among the store's more memorable Christmas Book extravagances.

★ WE INVENTED AMERICA'S ★
FAVORITE COCKTAIL

The margarita left the martini in the dust years ago as America's most popular cocktail. For that we owe a debt of thanks to a high school dropout named Mariano Martinez, who in 1971 converted a used soft-serve machine into a frozen-margarita maker at his struggling Tex-Mex restaurant in Dallas. "We were burning up blenders faster than I could afford to buy new ones," he says, and his bartenders couldn't keep up with orders. So he took matters into his own hands. Virtually overnight, the frozen margarita as we know it was born, and Tex-Mex cuisine would never be the same. Today Martinez's original margarita machine stands on display at the Smithsonian, and its inventor runs a successful restaurant mini-empire that employs more than six hundred people. The inspiration for Martinez's lightbulb moment? The 7-Eleven Slurpee machine, which, we're proud to say, was invented in Dallas, too.

★ WE'RE FAITHFUL ★
TO OUR LOCAL BRANDS

Shiner beer has been made in Shiner, Texas, since 1914, when a German immigrant named Kosmos Spoetzl took over the little town's brewing association. Today Spoetzl Brewery, one of only a handful of independent breweries to have survived Prohibition in Texas, is the fourth-largest craft brewer in the country and the oldest brewery of its kind in the state. Shiner Bock, its flagship beer, has gone from being an Austin-hippie cult favorite in the 1970s and '80s to being one of the best-loved craft beers in both the state and the country. That transformation owes largely to the efforts of a Mexican-born beer distributor named Carlos Alvarez, who saw the promise in Shiner's venerable reputation and old-world brewing methods. Today, Shiner beer is an object lesson for craft brewers all over the country. "They're sort of that next step up between a microbrewery and an Anheuser-Busch, and I think that's where all the microbreweries want to be someday," *Houston Press* food critic Robb Walsh told Public Media Texas in 2009. "They want to be like Shiner." Today the Spoetzl Brewery exports around 119,000 barrels of beer to other states each year, which seems like a lot until you realize that another 290,000 barrels stay right here in thirsty Texas.

Clockwise, from left: The Brewery in 1909, Kosmos Spoetzl, at right, and friends enjoy a few beers, the Shiner Bock logo.

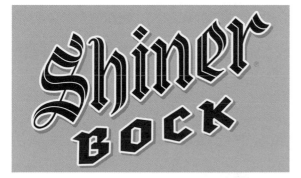

WE PUT THE "MICRO"
IN MICROELECTRONICS

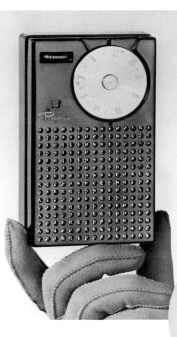

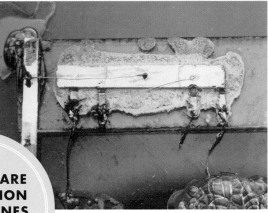

Opposite: Texas Instruments innovator Jack Kilby, surrounded by electronic devices at Texas Instruments headquarters. This page, left: Launched in 1954, the Regency TR-1 pocket radio revolutionized communications. Right: They didn't look like much, but Kilby's original 1958 integrated circuits set the stage for modern microchips and earned him a Nobel Prize.

TI CHIPS ARE IN 2 BILLION CELL PHONES AROUND THE WORLD.

The two game-changing-est breakthroughs in the history of consumer electronics and computing didn't happen in Silicon Valley. They happened in Dallas. The first came in 1954, in the form of the Regency TR-1, the first commercially available transistor radio. Produced by Texas Instruments, it weighed a half-pound, retailed for $49.95 (that's more than $400 in today's dollars, similar to the price of an iPhone today), and irreversibly changed the way people consumed music and broadcast media. Before the TR-1, the smallest portable radio was the size of a lunch box, required multiple (and multiple kinds of) batteries, and took ages to warm up. The TR-1 flicked to life instantly and could be carried around in your trouser pocket. The handheld radio became the most popular electronic communication device in history.

In 1958, just four years after Texas Instruments came out with the TR-1, a group of TI executives gathered in a room to get their first look at something one of their newest hires, Jack Kilby, had come up with while the rest of his colleagues were on summer vacation (poor Kilby hadn't earned any vacation days yet).

Kilby's invention was a $^7/_{15}$-by-$^1/_{16}$-inch sliver of germanium (a common semiconductor material at the time) with tiny filaments protruding from it. It was a crude-looking thing, but when Kilby hooked it up to an oscilloscope and his bosses saw a perfectly smooth sine wave, everyone knew history had been made. This was the first operational integrated circuit, or microchip. It effectively took the transistor, invented by Bell Labs in 1948, for a quantum leap, allowing semiconductor makers to place multiple transistors and other discrete electronic microcomponents on a single device, thus reducing the size of the circuit—and of the machines that relied on such circuitry—by an order of magnitude. Kilby's invention was more than a boon for the company he worked for, though it certainly was that; it was the first shot of the microelectronics revolution. Since 1961, when the integrated chip saw its first real-world applications (in military computers), the worldwide market for electronics using Kilby's basic technology has grown from $29 billion per year to some $1.5 trillion. Kilby's creation got him a Nobel Prize, and hopefully a few extra vacation days.

A BUSINESS MECCA FOR THE

As of 2012, a whopping fifty-two *Fortune* 500 companies called Texas home. Fifteen companies went public in Texas in 2011, making the Lone Star State the hottest IPO market in the country. What's more, those high-earning enterprises are spread across a wide range of sectors, from manufacturing to energy to telecommunications, strengthening Texas's growing reputation as one of the nation's most diversified state economies. But Texas's rise as a business magnet has to do with more than just how much or what a company makes. It has to do with how it does business. Of the "100 Best Companies to Work for in 2012," a list compiled by CNN-Money and *Fortune* magazine, twelve are headquarted in Texas. Better workplaces attract better talent, and better talent breeds better businesses. Suffice it to say, the future in Texas looks bright.

Texas IPOs, January 2011–March 2012
Initial Volume of Offer, in Millions of Dollars

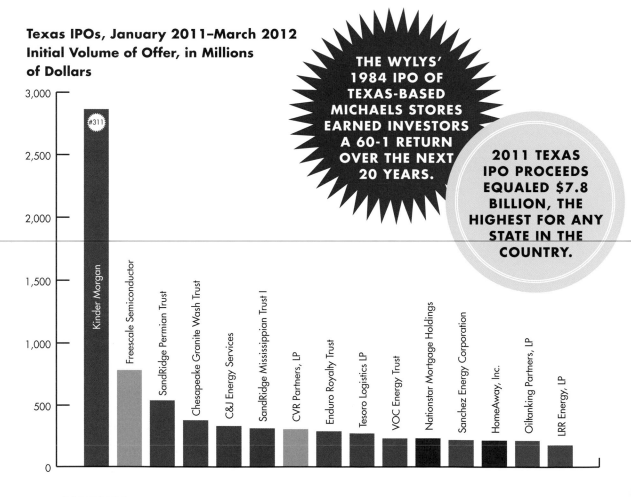

THE WYLYS' 1984 IPO OF TEXAS-BASED MICHAELS STORES EARNED INVESTORS A 60-1 RETURN OVER THE NEXT 20 YEARS.

2011 TEXAS IPO PROCEEDS EQUALED $7.8 BILLION, THE HIGHEST FOR ANY STATE IN THE COUNTRY.

Kinder Morgan · #311
Freescale Semiconductor
SandRidge Permian Trust
Chesapeake Granite Wash Trust
C&J Energy Services
SandRidge Mississippian Trust I
CVR Partners, LP
Enduro Royalty Trust
Tesoro Logistics LP
VOC Energy Trust
Nationstar Mortgage Holdings
Sanchez Energy Corporation
HomeAway, Inc.
Oiltanking Partners, LP
LRR Energy, LP

TOP TIER & UP-AND-COMING

**Annual Revenue, in Billions of Dollars,
of the 25 Top-Earning Companies in Texas**

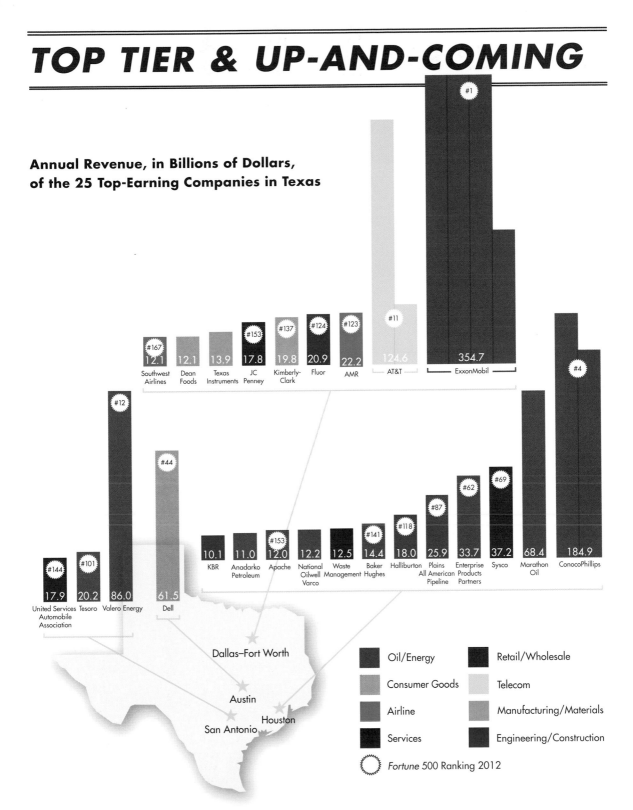

#1 ExxonMobil 354.7
#11 AT&T 124.6
#4 ConocoPhillips 184.9

#167 Southwest Airlines 12.1
Dean Foods 12.1
Texas Instruments 13.9
#153 JC Penney 17.8
#137 Kimberly-Clark 19.8
#124 Fluor 20.9
#123 AMR 22.2

#12 Valero Energy 86.0
#44 Dell 61.5
#144 United Services Automobile Association 17.9
#101 Tesoro 20.2

KBR 10.1
Anadarko Petroleum 11.0
#153 Apache 12.0
National Oilwell Varco 12.2
Waste Management 12.5
#141 Baker Hughes 14.4
#118 Halliburton 18.0
#87 Plains All American Pipeline 25.9
#62 Enterprise Products Partners 33.7
#69 Sysco 37.2
Marathon Oil 68.4

Dallas–Fort Worth
Austin
San Antonio
Houston

Oil/Energy
Consumer Goods
Airline
Services
Retail/Wholesale
Telecom
Manufacturing/Materials
Engineering/Construction

Fortune 500 Ranking 2012

CORPORATE CAPITAL
ON THE MOVE

So many people and companies are leaving the so-called Golden State for the Lone Star State these days that it's like the Gold Rush all over again, but with Texas standing in for California. Sure, both states are huge, with temperate climates, but the reason Texas has become such a magnet for West Coast businesses and human

capital is "not nature, but nurture," wrote Merrill Matthews, a resident scholar at the Institute for Policy Innovation, in the *New York Times*. Now, there's not a state in the union that doesn't trumpet itself as business-friendly, but here's the thing: Texas *walks the walk*. As Matthews and plenty of other experts have pointed out,

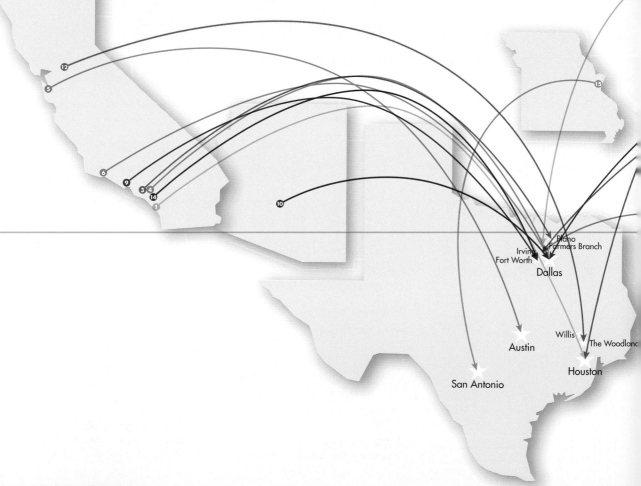

Texas's lower tax burden (there's no state income tax, period), its company- and worker-friendly regulatory environment, its affordable housing, its commitment to tort reform, its well-educated labor force, its welcoming attitude toward immigrants and migrants, and its plain old can-do spirit make this former Confederate-rebel state an entrepreneur's Shangri-La.

And California isn't the only blue state that's sending us its best and brightest. New York and Illinois have made some notable contributions recently, too. It's no coincidence that for eight years running, the editors of *Chief Executive* magazine have ranked Texas number one as the best state to do business in—and, as you might have guessed, California the worst.

● RETAIL/WHOLESALE

8. JC Penney
New York, NY, to Dallas, TX, in 1987.

9. Consolidated Electrical Distributors
Westlake Village, CA, to Irving, TX, in 2010.

● TRANSPORTATION

10. Greyhound Lines
Phoenix, AZ, to Dallas, TX, in 1987.

● WASTE MATERIALS

11. Waste Management
Chicago, IL, to Houston, TX, in 1998.

12. Waste Connections
Sacramento, CA, to The Woodlands, TX, in 2011.

● PAPER

13. Kimberly-Clark
Nennah, WI, to Farmers Branch, TX, in 1985.

● CONSTRUCTION

14. Fluor
Aliso Viejo, CA, to Dallas–Fort Worth, TX, in 2005.

● TELECOM

15. AT&T (formerly SBC)
St. Louis, MO, to San Antonio, TX, (and then Dallas, TX) in 1993.

● FOOD

1. Bubba Gump Shrimp
San Clemente, CA, to Houston, TX, in 2011.

● ENERGY

2. ExxonMobil
Trenton, NJ, to Irving, TX, in 1989.

3. Telmar Network Technology
Irvine, CA, to Plano, TX, in 2009.

● MEDICAL/HEALTH

4. Accent Meyers
Irvine, CA, to Dallas, TX, in 2011.

5. Arthro Care
Sunnyvale, CA, to Austin, TX, in 2004.

6. Tenet Healthcare
Santa Barbara, CA, to Dallas, TX, in 2004.

7. CCS Medical
Clearwater, FL, to Irving, TX, in 2011.

TEXAS GAME-CHANGER DELL INC.

When Michael Dell was twelve years old, he got into selling stamps. He started by getting the names of participants in local stamp auctions and then, banking on the hunch that more than a few of them would want to avoid the hassle of an auction, mailed them a twelve-page stamp catalog that he'd typed up himself. Only after an order came in from a collector did Dell go out and locate the stamps. He sold $2,000 worth of the collectibles in a matter of days and wasn't left with a bunch of stamps in search of a buyer.

A few years later, during his summer breaks from high school in the early '80s, Dell sold newspaper subscriptions. His job was to make cold calls from a phone list the newspaper subscription department provided. After a few dozen calls, Dell discerned a pattern: The people who bought subscriptions tended to be either newlyweds or new home buyers. So he hired some high school friends to ferret out names on marriage-license applications and mortgage filings in the sixteen counties surrounding Houston, and called those people instead of the ones on the cold lists. In a single summer he earned $18,000, more than the average teacher at his school.

When Dell was a freshman at the University of Texas, he started building and selling IBM PC–compatible computers built from stock components in his dorm room. A year later, in 1985, PCs Limited, as Michael Dell's venture was called at the time, came out with its first computer, the Turbo PC, which sold for $795. Instead of selling his machines in quarterly

installments to big-box stores or other intermediaries, as most PC companies were doing at the time, Dell advertised in computer magazines for sale directly to consumers. His fledgling company grossed more than $73 million in its first year of operation.

It's been said that Dell Inc. obeys three golden rules, and each one of them can be traced all the way back to Michael Dell's earliest forays into entrepreneurship. Foremost among those rules is "disdain inventory"—which is a good way to avoid having a ton of obsolete product sitting around when the next technological leap happens. Michael Dell understood that basic principle from the get-go, as his stamp-selling success proved. Golden rule number two: Listen to your customer. Dell Inc. pioneered the "configure-to-order" approach to computer manufacturing, allowing customers to customize a PC to their exact specifications. But listening to your customer goes beyond giving them what they ask for; it means knowing what they want before they know they want it—just as Dell knew that those newlyweds were going to want a newspaper subscription. Rule number three: Sell direct to the customer. Michael had figured that out in his college dorm room.

By 1992, Dell had become the youngest person ever to run a *Fortune* 500 company. In 1999 that company became the world's largest PC manufacturer. Soon its success gave rise to the term "the Dell effect," a phenomenon that *Fortune* magazine described succinctly in 2005: "The … computer maker spots a market where others are making fat profits, figures out how to deliver the same stuff for less, and then drains the profits right out of the pool."

Dell has distilled his M.O. down even further: "Since an early age," he's said, "I've been fascinated with the idea of eliminating unnecessary steps." He could have been talking about selling stamps or building servers, but either way his words point to a quality that unites him with Texans far and wide: that good old Lone Star resourcefulness.

Opposite: Michael Dell at his Austin plant in 1989. This page, top: Dell sits in the dorm room where he launched his enterprise at the University of Texas as the room's occupants, freshmen Russell Smith and Jacob Fruth, look on. Above: Teacher Chris Murray helps sixth-grade student Trinh Ha as she works with a Dell "netbook" during math class in Austin.

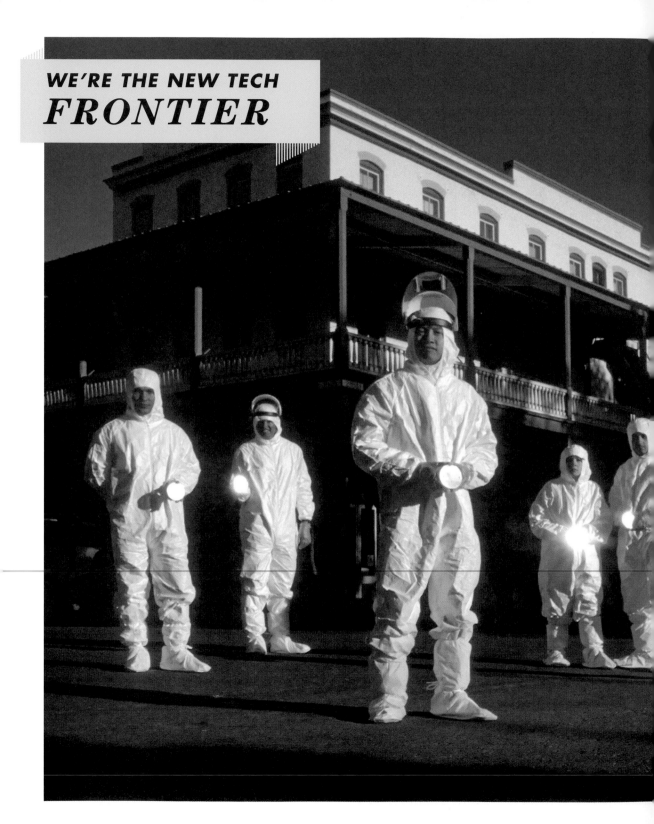

WE'RE THE NEW TECH FRONTIER

Austin is one of the world's most dynamic and fastest-growing tech-industry hubs, but it's not the next Silicon Valley. It doesn't want to be. Palo Alto and its surrounding Northern California communities may be crawling with just-out-of-college software developers brainstorming the next mobile app, but they're a volatile environment with massive turnover. "Silicon Valley is an acceleration machine for sure, but the downside is there can be a flight of talent…," said Mike Maples, a Palo Alto–based tech pioneer and financier who is now investing heavily in Austin, in an interview in 2010. "Austin is a better place to have a stable base of people working at a company." For one thing, young programmers and engineers can actually afford to live, and live well, in Austin, where the housing cost index is a whopping 300 percent lower than San Francisco's. For another, the tech industry—and thus the job market—in Austin is broad-based, spread across a wide portfolio of businesses of which e-commerce and social media are just two components. Bioscience, health-care, nanotechnology, robotics, semiconductors, IT software, clean energy—all these sectors help make up an incredibly vibrant and diverse landscape for tech professionals. Add to that a committed and innovative community of investors and advocates, including Austin Ventures, the largest noncoastal venture-capital firm in the U.S. Plus, there's the fact that the best and brightest of Silicon Valley flock to Austin every year for the city's South by Southwest Interactive conference, which is now the country's premier showcase for new consumer apps and software (see page 108).

THE A5 CHIPS IN APPLE IPHONES AND IPADS ARE MADE IN AUSTIN.

Workers sport "bunny suits"—worn in the "clean rooms" where microchips are made—in Old Town Austin. In chip manufacturing, invisible dust particles can ruin the circuitry, so such getups are crucial.

THE "NEXT BIG THING" TAKES OFF
FROM AUSTIN

Twitter didn't technically launch at Austin's South by Southwest Interactive conference in 2007, as has often been reported, but that five-day event is where the little tweeting bird found its wings. Over the course of the gathering, individual posts on the fledgling social-messaging service jumped from 20,000 per day to 60,000 per day, driven by a critical mass of tech-savvy conference-goers who saw the live plasma-screen feeds Twitter had set up in a main hallway and realized that the future would be a story told in 140 characters or less. Other tech innovators got the message. In 2009 another social-networking startup, Foursquare, chose SXSW for its market debut. Foursquare cofounder

Dennis Crowley described SXSW as the "perfect playground" for his location-based app's maiden outing. A year later, paying attendees at the Interactive component of the event alone jumped to 13,000, 40 percent more than in 2009, and more than paid to attend SXSW's live-band showcase, which was what started the festival in the first place, back in 1987, when it was just a laid-back music fair. In 2011, SXSWi attendance jumped to 20,000, tech blogs and magazines were calling the event the hottest tech gathering of the year, and software engineers at start-ups and tech giants alike were racing to finish new apps before the start of the conference.

KATY PERRY, JAMES BLUNT, AND JOHN MAYER ARE AMONG THE SUPERSTARS WHO WERE DISCOVERED AT SXSW.

Opposite: Crowds gather in the Austin Convention Center for South by Southwest, 2012. This page, top: Laptops are a common sight at the conference, which brought about $168 million into the Austin economy in 2011. Bottom, left and right: In addition to countless impromptu performances, 2,286 musical acts, performing on 104 stages around the city, were featured in 2012, including 547 international acts from 49 foreign countries.

LEADING *THE NATION* OUT

While other states got knocked flat by the recent economic crisis and are still struggling, Texas bounced back and did so faster and stronger than almost any other state. In fact, Texas actually ended up gaining jobs during the Great Recession—the only one of the twenty most populous states to do so—and has posted more new net jobs since the start of the downturn than all of the other states *combined*. The reasons behind Texas's astounding resilience and recovery are the same ones that are making the state an economic juggernaut today: a strong energy and exports sector anchoring a broad-based economic portfolio; a robust but stable housing market that neither boomed nor crashed, thanks in part to shrewd, conservative lending practices; and a virtuous cycle of population growth fueling demand, which in turn creates more jobs.

**Distribution of Jobs
Added Nationwide
Since December 2007**

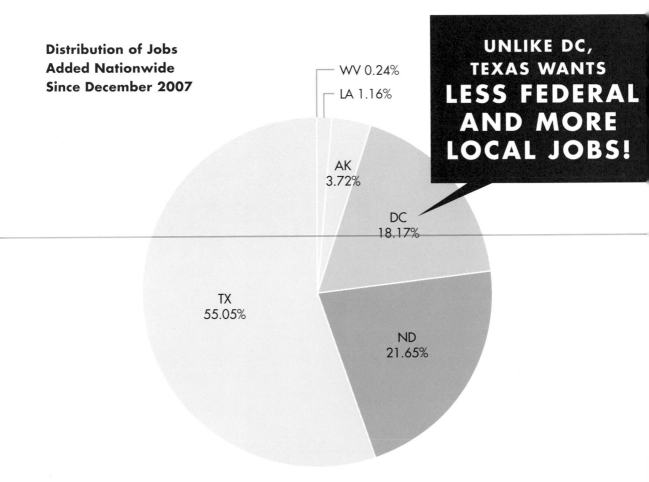

WV 0.24%

LA 1.16%

AK 3.72%

DC 18.17%

TX 55.05%

ND 21.65%

UNLIKE DC, TEXAS WANTS LESS FEDERAL AND MORE LOCAL JOBS!

OF RECESSION

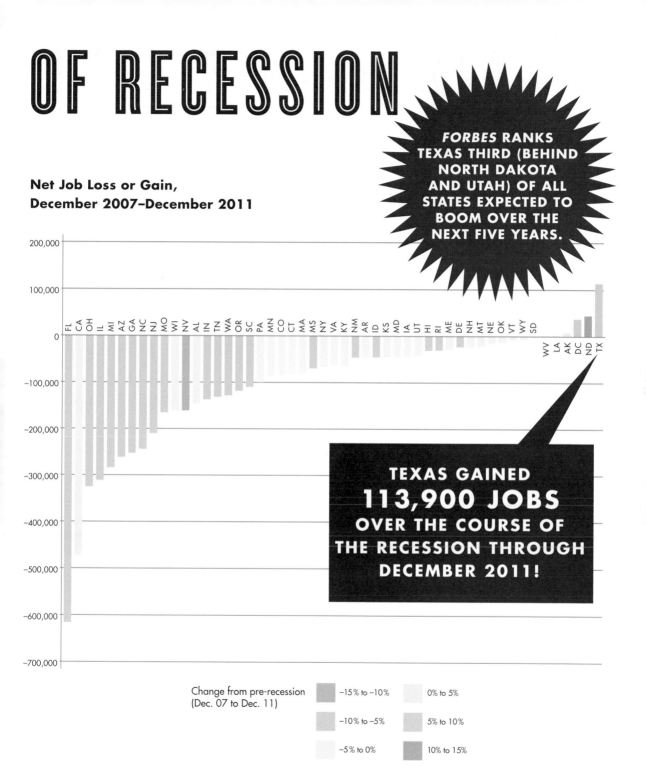

Net Job Loss or Gain,
December 2007–December 2011

FORBES RANKS TEXAS THIRD (BEHIND NORTH DAKOTA AND UTAH) OF ALL STATES EXPECTED TO BOOM OVER THE NEXT FIVE YEARS.

TEXAS GAINED
113,900 JOBS
OVER THE COURSE OF THE RECESSION THROUGH DECEMBER 2011!

Change from pre-recession
(Dec. 07 to Dec. 11)

- −15% to −10%
- −10% to −5%
- −5% to 0%
- 0% to 5%
- 5% to 10%
- 10% to 15%

EVEN OUR PREACHERS ARE
ENTREPRENEURS

"I have talked to several farmers here about the tithes in England, and they laugh." Those words, quoted in the book *The Churching of America, 1776–2005*, were contained in a letter the English journalist William Cobbett wrote to his friends back home about churchgoing in rural America in the early 19th century. The Oxfordshire native just couldn't believe that in America farmers didn't have to give 10 percent of their crop to the church like they did in old England—and yet the people built churches anyhow, and darn nice ones. That's a Texas-style lesson for you: Let folks worship as they please and churches will grow and prosper of their own free will.

Texans have taken the free-market approach to religion to unsurpassed heights. Just look at the ministry of T.D. Jakes, the chief pastor of the Potter's House, a come-one-come-all megachurch in Dallas. He has a congregation of 30,000, dozens of bestselling books, his own record label, a movie-production company, and a shining trail of good works stretching from America's inner cities to the slums of Nairobi. The Reverend Jakes is living proof that Texas is not only the best state in which to build a company, but also the best state in which to build a church. This West Virginia–born son of a teacher and a janitor got his start in a storefront in Montgomery, West

Virginia, where he had a side job digging ditches to make ends meet. It wasn't until 1996, after he'd moved his and fifty other church families to Dallas, that his vision for a megachurch took shape. Today Jakes's sermons emphasize the God-given right to prosper as a pillar of Christian ministry.

Jakes has kindred spirits down in Houston, including Reverend Ed Young, of the 24,000-strong Second Baptist Church, and Joel Osteen, the pastor of Lakewood Church—the largest single congregation in the United States. A former TV technician with a high school education, Osteen now shepherds a flock of 7 million people a week through his television ministry alone. It is the most-watched religious broadcast in America. You don't see any crosses or icons at Osteen's services, but you do see 16,000 or so very motivated people of every age and color who don't look at all put out to be up early on a weekend receiving a gospel of growth, optimism, and self-improvement. As if Osteen alone didn't provide enough star power, in 2002 Lakewood brought on board Marcos Witt, a singer and four-time Latin Grammy winner, to lead the church's 40,000 Spanish-speaking congregants.

Roughly 65 percent of Texas residents belong to an organized religious body, 10 percent more than the U.S. population at large, and 70 percent consider religion to be "very important." And while megachurches have made a big impact in large cities, small, community-based places of worship remain a cornerstone of everyday life for millions of Texans. For them, attending worship regularly isn't just about piety and individual redemption, though that's certainly a strong thread in religious observance among many Texans, as it is all across the South. It's also about a sense of belonging, of wanting to be engaged, of wanting to improve life for the whole community.

Clockwise from far left: T.D. Jakes preaches to a packed Potter's House in 2006; the Reverend Jakes preaches passionately; Joel Osteen in 2005; Marcos Witt celebrates his 2004 Grammy win for *Recordando Otra Vez*.

WE GOT RELIGION
(IN EVERY FLAVOR)

Texans are churchgoers. The city of Lubbock, in West Texas, is said to have more churches per capita than any other town in the country. Texas ranks first in the nation in the number of Evangelical Protestants, second in Mainline Protestants, and third in Catholics. And the numbers are growing: Churches in the state reported an increase in membership of 2.17 million between 2000 and 2010. We're mosque-goers and temple-goers, too. Texas has nearly half a million practicing Muslims, and at least thirty-four separate Hindu congregations serving some 60,000 worshippers, plus another 60,000 practicing Jews and even more practicing Buddhists. We've got Mennonites, Lutherans, Zoroastrians, Quakers, Episcopalians, and pretty much every other denomination and subdenomination you can think of. And

while megachurches get a lot of attention in places like Dallas and Houston (see page 112), religious life in most of the state still revolves around small houses of worship serving their immediate community. A full 70 percent of Baptist congregations in Texas have fewer than 100 regular worshippers. In Texas, we like to think big, but on Sundays we still like to get to know our neighbor.

Opposite, clockwise from left: Mission Church in El Paso; Second Church of Christ, Scientist in Fort Worth; Cestohowa Church in Cestohowa; Church Fort Stockton in West Texas. This page, clockwise from top left: An early photo taken outside the chapel at Mo-Ranch Presbyterian Conference Center in Kerr County; Risin Sun Cowboy Church in East Texas; Pleasant Grove Baptist Church in Freestone County; Plano Masjid mosque in Plano; Zephyr Gospel Tabernacle in Zephyr; Barsana Dham Temple near Austin; Congregation Beth Jacob in Galveston.

TEXANS ARE CHART-TOPPERS
(AND WE CAME UP WITH THE CHART)

Texas—the state that gave the world Janis Joplin, Beyoncé, Willie Nelson, and Buddy Holly—has been ahead of the curve in popular music since the 1940s, when DJs in the state helped pioneer the then-novel idea of audience-driven radio programming. The first radio-station music survey in the country took place at KXOL in Fort Worth in 1955, and even before that, in Dallas, Gordon McClendon of KLIF was poring over the sales receipts of record stores around the city in order to come up with on-air playlists that reflected teenage listening tastes. His station was one of the earliest adopters of the jukebox-driven Top 40 format, and by the mid-1950s was the highest-rated metropolitan radio station in the United States. Texas notched many radio firsts in the postwar era, in fact, including the first Spanish-language and Mexican-American-owned station (KCOR, established in San Antonio in 1946) and one of the first black DJs (at KNUZ/KQUE in Houston). Radio formatting has changed a lot since then, but Texas is still producing a disproportionate share of chart-toppers and—with Austin's annual South by Southwest festival (see page 108) and the groundbreaking PBS music showcase *Austin City Limits*—is still a music leader.

The "CHIRPING" CRICKETS

Opposite: Beyoncé Knowles performs at the 2011 MTV Video Music Awards. This page: With their 1957 debut, Buddy Holly's group the Crickets became teen favorites—something Dallas DJ Gordon McClendon surely made note of. Other Texas music greats include Willie Nelson, Selena, and Norah Jones.

PEARSALL'S GEORGE STRAIT HAS MORE #1 HIT SINGLES THAN ANY ARTIST IN HISTORY.

WE INVENTED THE DANCE HALL

"Dance halls will get in your blood," wrote the musician Pat Green about Texas's legendary small-town music venues in the book *Dance Halls and Dreamers*. "If you are not from here, it will take you a minute to let it get a hold of you. But I guarantee if you let it get a hold of you, you will never want it to let go." True words indeed. For generations of Texans, going to the local dance hall is just what you did on a Saturday night. These places, jumping with a style of country music that migrated to Texas from Tennessee and other corners of Appalachia, have long been the heart of rural life in the Lone Star State, just like honky-tonks are in the towns. Places like Gilley's in Pasadena, Texas—made famous by the 1980 John Travolta movie *Urban Cowboy*—may have put Texas boot-scootin' (and mechanical-bull riding) on the national map for a little while, but really, Texas dance halls are all about

history. Over the years they've been incubators for scores of country-music greats, from Ernest Tubb and Lefty Frizzell to Willie Nelson. They're also about entrepreneurship: The first dance halls were built by small-town business owners who saw a need in their community and filled it. It took savvy and hard work to run a good dance hall, and still does. Many of these creaky old wood-floored joints have given up the ghost since their heyday in the early 20th century, but others are being restored and revived, both by nonprofits and by entrepreneurs who see the promise of livelihood in these places just as their predecessors did a century ago.

The Broken Spoke in Austin, pictured here, is one of countless Texas dance halls. Other iconic spots: Billy Bob's in Fort Worth, Gruene Hall in New Braunfels, Sons of Hermann Hall in Dallas, and Schroeder Hall in Goliad—to name just a few.

Even when Top 40 radio was still in its infancy, another music-biz first was in the offing in the Lone Star State. This one was the brainchild of a former high school football player and DJ from Beaumont, Texas, named J. P. Richardson, who called himself the Big Bopper. In 1958, buoyed by the success of his B-side hit "Chantilly Lace," the Bopper hired a camera crew to record him performing that song and two others on something called magnetic videotape—a medium that had been introduced only a couple of years earlier. He hammed it up for the camera, using simple props like an old-fashioned tele- phone (on which he engaged in playful pillow-talk banter between verses), and lip-synched the lyrics. In so doing, he created the first rock video—a term coined by the Big Bopper himself.

IN MAY 1957, THE BIG BOPPER SET A RECORD FOR CONTINUOUS BROADCASTING: FIVE DAYS, TWO HOURS, AND EIGHT MINUTES.

...AND THE MUSIC VIDEO

Left: A rare album cover from 1959. Above: Decades before MTV, the Big Bopper shot visual accompaniments—later called music videos—for three songs in 1958.

TEXAS GAME-CHANGER
HALF PRICE BOOKS

Texas's entrepreneurial lore often seems dominated by the Big Rich of wildcatters, oil barons, and high-tech giants, but Ken Gjemre and Patricia Anderson proved that in this state you can also build a business empire on pure idealism.

They are the founders of the largest family-owned bookstore chain in the country, Half Price Books, which started its life in a converted Laundromat on Lover's Lane in Dallas in 1972, with an inventory of two thousand titles (mostly from their own shelves) and a mission not just to sell books at a discount, but also to preserve trees, extend book life, and promote literacy. Their corporate motto was "Waste not, and read a lot," and their sales slogan was "We'll buy and sell everything printed except yesterday's newspaper."

Were Gjemre and Anderson hippies? To the very core. Gjemre owned a peace sign–emblazoned Volkswagen bus. They vocally opposed the Vietnam War, wrote for underground newspapers, and marched for free speech. And yet Anderson was a coal miner's daughter and Gjemre had won a Silver Star in World War II. "Ken wasn't just an observer of the peace movement," said Sharon Anderson Wright, the daughter of Pat Anderson and HPB's current president and CEO. "He had been shaped by that destruction, so when he met my mother they began to advocate for peace and the environment."

Gjemre and Anderson were true believers—a breed that Texans have always taken kindly to—and they channeled their beliefs into that most Texan of undertakings: growing a business. It's what's so special about them, and about the institution they created: They went big—100 stores in sixteen states and counting—because they simply wanted to do more good for more people. "They didn't start with the idea of opening a chain of bookstores," says Wright, who has worked for her mother's company since she was thirteen years old. "Their aim was just to provide affordable books for everybody."

There has been no formal science to the company's expansion, which continues to spring from the founders' free-press ideals. "We all love books," says Wright. "We all love literature and art and music.

As the media to deliver them have expanded, so have our offerings." Stores in some towns were opened simply because an employee wanted to move there. Lots of second- and third-generation workers, extended family, and aging hippies are still with the company today. The founders' aversion to borrowing even a cent has meant that growth is funded solely from profits. Add to that a keen resourcefulness born of thrift. The recession that began in 2008 caused real estate prices to slide nationwide, a circumstance that enabled HPB to move into new cities and to open stores in better areas of cities where the company was already established.

Today, Half Price Books employs nearly three thousand people from all walks of life. "We have writers, artists, teachers, bartenders," says Wright. "What draws them is the fact that every day they come in is going to be interesting.... You're interacting with people all day long. You're talking about books.... There is a lot of diversity and great freedom to be exactly who you are." There is also a famously good benefits package and little staff turnover. HPB veterans have been known to announce to new employees, "You haven't been hired, you've been adopted."

There was belt-tightening during the recession, sure, but employee benefits have remained inviolate, as have HPB's philanthropic endeavors. The company continues to give away more than 2 million books a year to schools, libraries, hospitals, clinics, shelters, and community centers, both in America and overseas.

Half Price Books is not straying from the path its founders laid out. A future IPO is not in the cards. "I don't want anybody to tell me what to do," says Wright, echoing her mother's sentiments. "It would ruin the culture and the company, and I'd feel like an ass for the rest of my life."

Opposite: Cofounder Ken Gjemre in 1988, sampling the merchandise. This page, top: Wright had electric car chargers installed at Half Price's flagship location on Northwest Highway in Dallas. Middle: The original store on Lover's Lane. Bottom: Cofounder Pat Anderson with Wright.

WE LIKE TEARING DOWN FENCES, NOT PUTTING 'EM UP

Texas's Twenty-Third Congressional District stretches some six hundred miles from the outskirts of El Paso to the edge of San Antonio and on almost to Corpus Christi, encompassing most of our state's border with Mexico. It's got no big cities, two military bases, and lots of jackrabbits and lizards. Two-thirds of its people are Mexican-American—including the district's third-generation Mexican-American congressman, Quico Canseco. The towns on the Mexico side of the border have a long history of revolt against Mexico City, which puts them in good company with rebellious Texas. Those towns are twinned with sister cities on the Texas side of the border through skeins of kinship and economic ties that connect thousands of families and small businesses on both sides of the Rio Grande. Overwhelmingly, these border towns, as well as most Texans, including Governor Rick Perry, opposed the security wall proposed by the feds in 2008. Indeed, the border in this part of Texas is an illusory thing, an arbitrary line that plunges through the center of what the social historian Colin Woodard calls El Norte, one of the stateless cultural "nations" that have long defined public life in North America (see page 28). In this respect, the Twenty-Third, which seems to have less of everything than its neighbors except empty land, is the most richly Texan of places, because the people who live there know that opportunity resides in what unites us and not what divides us.

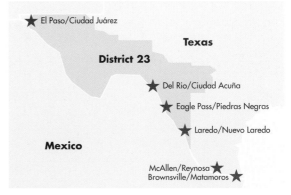

Left: View of the Rio Grande from a hilltop in Big Bend Ranch State Park. Above: Canseco's district and its border towns.

WE SEE BEAUTY IN THE
WILDEST PLACES

Back in the 1970s, when the minimalist artist Donald Judd moved to the remote West Texas town of Marfa, no one could have imagined that this former railroad watering stop would become a contemporary-art mecca—a mandatory pilgrimage site for every art maven and gallery owner east of the Hudson River. Today Marfa, population 2,000 or so, is home to Judd's Chinati Foundation and Museum, his vast land-art installations, multiple galleries, and one of the most curiously diverse groups of small-town dwellers anywhere. Older-generation Marfans were no strangers to outsiders seeking to realize a vision here; the film director George Stevens chose Marfa as the location for his 1956 epic *Giant*, imprinting the West Texas high desert on the American imagination. The locals welcomed Stevens and his cast—Elizabeth Taylor and James Dean among them—just as they did Judd and his successors. Today, all that artistic ferment is creeping out of Marfa proper and into the vast expanses of Chihuahuan desert that surround it. The "Prada store" pictured opposite—a 15-by-25-foot cube of adobe, plaster, and glass—isn't a store at all but rather an artwork that the Berlin-based artists Michael Elmgreen and Ingar Dragset installed on a patch of scrubland some twenty-six miles outside of Marfa. The artists intend to leave their creation to succumb to the desert over time—just like Reata, the false-front Victorian mansion depicted in *Giant*, is doing today—ultimately returning it to the gorgeous empty canvas from which it sprang.

This page: A selection of 15 untitled concrete works by Judd sits permanently in a tall field of prairie grass. Opposite, clockwise from top left: Judd in Marfa, 1966; the Reata mansion, constructed for the set of *Giant*, was left to decompose in the desert after production was complete—a beautiful and haunting testament to the film; James Dean and Elizabeth Taylor in *Giant* (1956); like the Reata ruins, this Prada store installation is intended to never be repaired, so it will slowly degrade back into the natural landscape.

TWO FILMS—
THERE WILL BE BLOOD
AND *NO COUNTRY
FOR OLD MEN*—
NOMINATED FOR BEST
PICTURE AT THE 2008
ACADEMY AWARDS
WERE FILMED
IN MARFA.

WE HARNESSED THE
HIGH PLAINS

The Republic of Texas and later the young state of Texas didn't have any money, but it did have a lot of land. In fact, the birth of modern Texas is really the story of how Texans parlayed all that land into capital and power. A compelling chapter in that story concerns the XIT Ranch, which at its peak in the 1880s covered 3 million acres of high plains in the Texas Panhandle and was home to 150,000 head of cattle. It was at the time the largest contiguous swath of land under fence in the world. (The name, it is said, stands for "Ten in Texas," because the ranch covered ten counties.) The 200-mile-long strip of rangeland had been sold in 1882 to British investors to raise money for the construction of a new capitol building in Austin. The magnificent capitol, with its soaring pink-granite dome, was completed in 1888 and is fifteen feet taller than the capitol dome in Washington, D.C.

But the fate of the XIT Ranch itself is the more revealing part of this story. At the end of the century, as the era of cattle drives drew to a close and settlers began to populate the Panhandle, the owners of the XIT sold off their holdings in ever more valuable parcels, giving the Brits a handsome return on their bet. In 1921, the first Panhandle oil well came in, bringing wealth to the once desolate reaches of the high plains. Today, those wind-scoured plains have borne

fruit again: The Panhandle is home to some of the world's largest wind farms, making this corner of Texas the wind-power capital of the state, which in turn is the wind-power capital of the country (see page 84). It may seem a far cry from the Panhandle's cowboy days, but it's not: People there are doing what they've always done—using the resources at hand to propel Texas into the future.

Opposite: Water-pumping windmills in the Panhandle. This page, left and below right, top and bottom: Other Panhandle activities include hay baling, cotton growing, and oil drilling. Below left: A late-19th-century map shows counties, railroad lines, and land owned by the "Capital Company" (XIT Ranch).

IN THE 1880s, THE 3 MILLION–ACRE XIT RANCH WAS THE WORLD'S LARGEST FENCED RANGE.

SKETCH MAP OF THE PAN HANDLE OF TEXAS.

WE MAKE THE MOST OF OUR COAST

"Galveston, oh Galveston, I still
Hear your sea winds blowin'
I still see her dark eyes glowin'
She was 21
When I left Galveston."

— Glen Campbell

Texas doesn't squander an inch of its 367 miles of Gulf Coast (really, more like 3,300 miles when you include all the inlets, bays, and river mouths), which boast one of the most diverse mixed-use stretches of seashore in the country. Tourism, fishing, shrimping, petroleum refining, cruise-ship ports, avian

wintering grounds—all these constituent parts coexist harmoniously along the Texas Riviera under the stewardship of the Texas General Land Office, which manages the region's natural resources and promotes the efficient and equitable use of waterfront public property. And in Texas, a nice walk along the beach is a constitutional right, enforced by the Texas Land Office. Thanks to the Open Beaches Act, passed in 1959, the public has free and unrestricted access to every inch of beachfront along Texas's coast, whether it's privately owned or not. (California tried to pass its own version of this law, but they California-ized the teeth right out of it, requiring complex layers of

city and county approvals and endless vetting by the California Coastal Commission.) What's more, coastal cities like Galveston and Corpus Christi, which have come back bigger and better after some of the most destructive hurricanes of the modern era, stand as towering symbols of Texan resilience. With its broad-based economy and open-to-all environment, Texas's Gulf Coast is a microcosm of Texas itself.

Opposite: The Bob Hall pier on Padre Island is a favorite spot for Gulf Coast fishermen. This page, clockwise from top left: A tanker navigates near Galveston; fishing trawlers in Port Isabel; the world's only naturally wild population of whooping cranes winters along the Texas Gulf Coast; sunset over the Corpus Christi refineries; fish hanging in Port Aransas.

FARMING FOR THE NATION

Agriculture is the second-biggest industry in Texas after petroleum and natural gas; farming generates more than $80 billion a year in revenue. The Lone Star State is the biggest agricultural force in the country: It has more acreage devoted to farming than any other state and boasts the most revenue from livestock farming. We lead the nation in the production of cattle, cotton, and sheep, among other commodities, and we rank in the top five for scores of others. Our farming industry is shouldered in large part by small, independent growers. Only 0.3 percent of Texas farms are owned by nonfamily corporations. Over half are smaller than 100 acres, and more than 85 percent of them are run by families or family-run partnerships.

Types of Texas Farms

■ Individual/Family
■ Family Corporations
□ Partnerships
■ Nonfamily corporations
▨ Other (estate, trust, institutional)

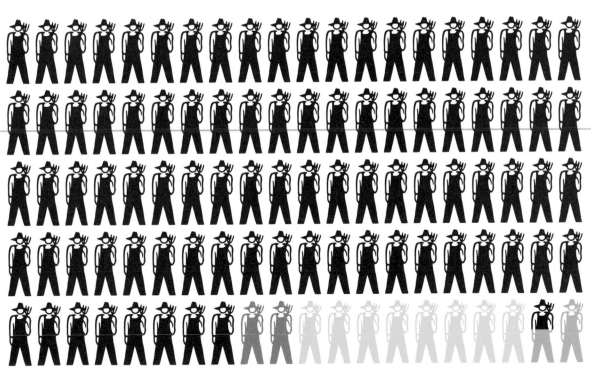

Top Texas Agricultural Products, with National Ranking

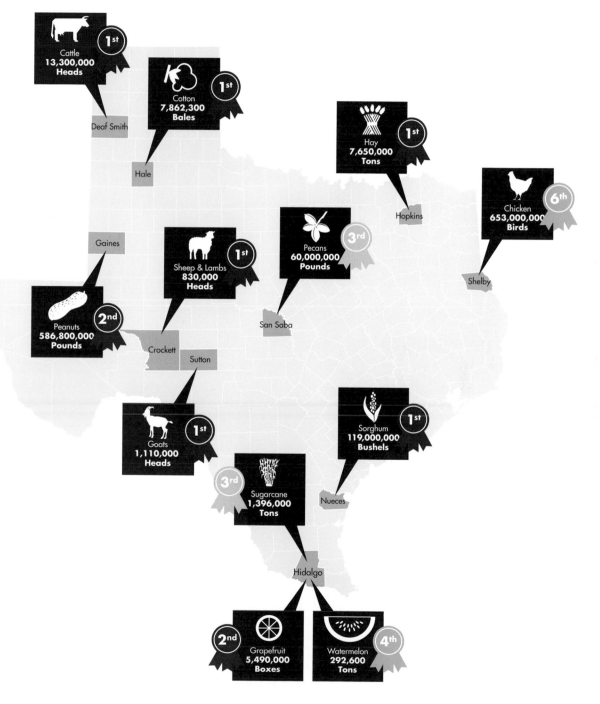

Cattle
**13,300,000
Heads**
1st

Deaf Smith

Cotton
**7,862,300
Bales**
1st

Hale

Hay
**7,650,000
Tons**
1st

Hopkins

Chicken
**653,000,000
Birds**
6th

Shelby

Gaines

Sheep & Lambs
**830,000
Heads**
1st

Pecans
**60,000,000
Pounds**
3rd

San Saba

Peanuts
**586,800,000
Pounds**
2nd

Crockett

Sutton

Goats
**1,110,000
Heads**
1st

Sorghum
**119,000,000
Bushels**
1st

Nueces

Sugarcane
**1,396,000
Tons**
3rd

Hidalgo

Grapefruit
**5,490,000
Boxes**
2nd

Watermelon
**292,600
Tons**
4th

WE SEE THE FOREST FOR
THE TREES

Among the oil tycoons, land speculators, cotton kings, and cattle men, the great Texas lumber barons are often forgotten. And unjustly. From the 1880s through the Depression, the virgin pinelands of East Texas fell to the saw and ax at an extraordinary clip, as new railroad lines created markets for lumber in every corner of the state, whose infrastructure—from houses to oil derricks—still relied heavily on wood. Fortunes were made from the great East Texas sawmills, the biggest of which could turn out hundreds of thousands of board feet of lumber a day. Men like John Martin Thompson, Joseph Kurth Sr., and W.T. Joyce presided over vast, lucrative milling operations deep in the eastern forests, where mill-company towns popped up like saplings. John Henry Kirby, the son of East Texas farmers in hardscrabble Tyler County, built a lumber empire that eventually held the surface rights to a million acres in Southeast Texas, earning Kirby the sobriquet "Prince of the Pines."

The Piney Woods bonanza drew to a close toward the middle of the 20th century. Most assumed that the land the loggers left behind would be given over to farming, but it turned out that the soil of the pinelands wasn't so good for planting and tilling. What it was good for was growing more southern yellow pines. Soon, people like

EACH YEAR, TEXAS PLANTS 100 MILLION SEEDLINGS— ROUGHLY FIVE PER TEXAN.

W. Goodrich Jones, a banker in East Texas, realized that conservation of the forests and the revival of those woodlands already logged were going to be crucial to the future economic well-being of East Texas. In 1914, Jones, who had spent a formative two years in the magnificent Black Forest of Germany, and a group of fellow conservationists founded the Texas Forestry Association. At their urging, the state of Texas created a department of forestry the following year. It urged lumber companies to practice selective cutting and sustainable logging. In 1933, seeing the immense mutual benefit of setting aside future timberland, Texas, which was unique among states in retaining full control of all its public lands, passed a law that allowed the U.S. Forest Service to purchase logged tracts in the state, and those lands became vast national forests. Then, in the 1940s, Texas became home to the first tree-farming movement in the country; it helped landowners plant and grow trees and maintain viable timberland. By the mid-1980s, more than 2,500 privately owned tree farms were operating in Texas. Today, in a typically Texan triumph of pragmatism over ideology, the conservation movement and the lumber industry have found a common cause in the long-term health of Texas's mighty trees.

Top: Log-skidding teams from the Southern Pine Lumber Company, 1903. Left: Seedlings grown at this West Texas nursery are sold for planting in large-scale conservation projects.

TEXAS GAME-CHANGER
TEXAS A&M

"Give me an army of West Point graduates and I'll win the battle. Give me a handful of Texas Aggies, and I'll win the war."
—General George S. Patton

Aggies constituted by far the biggest contingent of World War II officers from a single college—more than those from West Point and Annapolis *combined*. Of those 14,000-plus Aggie officers, twenty-nine were generals. Seven Aggies received the Medal of Honor. This was par for the course for the Agricultural and Mechanical College of Texas. The mission of serving and defending our country has been integral to this school since its birth in 1876. It's a very Texan notion: that a college or university should do more than merely exchange classroom instruction for tuition fees, funneling graduates out into the world to earn their living. It should produce good citizens and great soldiers—men and women trained not just in the vocation that supports their livelihood, but in duty, honor, and country.

A&M began as a land-grant college after the Civil War and is now one of the largest public research universities in the country, but the Corps is still America's biggest student group in uniform outside of the armed forces service academies and still supplies the military with lots of commissioned officers. Moreover, the Corps remains a driving force in the spirit of the student body.

Today A&M has one of the largest college campuses in the world—with more than 50,000 full-time students studying every imaginable subject and representing all fifty states and 130 countries—but its historical role as an agriculture school continues to instill in those students small-town values geared toward community and tradition. Indeed, you'd be hard-pressed to find another college or university where ritual and tradition are more enthusiastically observed—from the annual bonfire (held off-campus since 2002) to the musters that bring students and faculty together to remember Aggies who have died in the past year. If you've ever gone to an Aggies football game and wondered why no one ever sits down, that's just an Aggie's way of honoring the "12th man"—that ever-ready fan who is prepared to jump

onto the gridiron at any moment if his team can't field the required eleven players. And then there's the Aggie ring, worn with pride by countless alumni since the 1880s. One such alumnus tells the story of falling on hard times and having to pawn his Aggie ring, only to get it back in the mail from the pawn-shop owner, also an A&M grad, who refused to accept any money in return.

Perhaps what's most remarkable about Texas A&M is not how tradition-bound it is, but how forward-looking it is. In 2006, it began explicitly stating in its hiring and promotion policy that technology com-mercialization is a criterion to be considered when granting tenure. That put real-world value on an aca-demic's achievements and empowered faculty to advance their careers in ways that also bolstered the university's partnerships with innovative industries. The move built on an extraordinary record of hiring, graduating, and cultivating visionary researchers and engineers, including Norman Borlaug, winner of the Nobel Peace Prize in 1970 for crop-productivity inno-

vations that saved more than a billion lives in poor nations. Simply put, an Aggie is self-reliant, forever an optimist, and pragmatic and sentimental in equal measure—which is another way of saying that an Aggie is just a good Texan.

Opposite: Mounted Cavalry units have played a central role in A&M traditions. This page, above: The Aggie Band spells out its support for the "12th Man" in 1984. Below: Agronomist Norman Borlaug with some of the Mexican field technicians who helped him produce improved wheat varieties, circa 1952.

Texans don't place a lot of stock in political and cultural labels. Maybe that's because we have such an uncanny knack for defying them. Just look at John Mackey, the founder and co-CEO of Whole Foods Markets, the $10 billion Austin-based grocery chain. Few entrepreneurs have made such a seemingly stark about-face—from anticorporate granola peddler to anti-regulation free-market guru—in the span of a single, contiguous career. And yet he's basically been the same guy all along.

When the natural-foods shop he and his girlfriend opened in an old Victorian house in Austin in the late 1970s started losing money, Mackey decided that was unacceptable. And anyhow, there were a dozen other musty little stores like his around Austin already. So he grew his business, borrowing $45,000 from friends and family and launching the first Safer Way (which would go on to become Whole Foods Market), which opened in Austin in 1980. It sold bulk grains and the like, but it also sold beer and coffee and had the clean, well-lighted vibe of, well, a supermarket. The store earned a profit immediately. Sure, Mackey was a longhair who'd lived in a food co-op, but in his chest beat the heart of a competitive entrepreneur who would go on to exemplify the quintessentially Texan motto "Go big or go home."

Today, Whole Foods Market employs some 64,000 people and operates more than three hundred stores, and Mackey is one of the world's most outspoken advocates of what he calls "conscious capitalism"—a movement that could be best defined as "be like Whole Foods." For twelve years running, the enterprise has been rated one of the "100 Best Companies to Work for" by *Fortune* magazine. Employees enjoy a workplace that promotes a healthy lifestyle and long-term investment in their careers. Mackey flies coach, pays himself $1 a year, and enforces a salary cap on his executives, who can make no more than nineteen times the average worker's check. He is surrounded by believers: No one on his executive team has left in more than eleven years.

In short, Mackey is a good-hearted, fleece-wearing, very well-off lefty. Well, not quite. Remember what we said about Texans and labels? Suffice it to say that Berkeley or Portland would probably never produce a natural-foods champion who preaches against government-mandated health-care and forced unionization, as Mackey did in the *Wall Street Journal* in 2009. His article angered a lot of people, but he is not shy.

What gave Mackey's opinions extra weight was

the fact that he was speaking not as a pundit but as a hardworking CEO who has had to make payroll every month for more than thirty years. Regarding the right-to-work law, which Texas has and which Mackey is for, he's pointed out that while he can't prevent anyone from unionizing, none of his employees—unlike those of countless other grocery chains—have ever bothered. Whole Foods' deal is better: "We have better benefits and higher pay." Whole Foods' highly successful low-premium/high-deductible health-care plan includes excellent incentives for wellness, including personal health savings accounts. The company contributes every year for every employee, including lots of part-timers.

In 2011, Mackey wrote another op-ed piece for the *Journal*, this one focused on the most urgent subject of the day: job creation. "Business is not a zero-sum game struggling over a fixed pie," he said. "Instead it grows and makes the total pie larger, creating value for all of its major stakeholders—customers, employees, suppliers, investors, and communities." This was simply common sense, applied to the common good, which is what John Mackey has been about from the start.

Mackey lounges in the produce section at Whole Foods in Austin, 2009.

GOD GAVE US BLACK-EYED PEAS AND
WE MADE CAVIAR

There may be no food on earth whose deliciousness exceeds the sum of its parts more than the chicken-fried steak. This Texas specialty—the invention of which has been variously ascribed to 19th-century chuck-wagon cooks and Depression-era German immigrants—is a marvel of Lone Star resourcefulness. You take a tough, unloved cut of beef like cube steak and pound it with something flat and heavy until the meat is tender and as thin as a wafer. Then you dredge it, bread it, and fry it in a skillet with plenty of fat, just as you would if you were making southern fried chicken, which is where the dish gets its name. The result is a luscious, savory piece of

protein that has sustained generations of hungry Texans in diners and dining rooms across the state.

Texas's vast tapestry of native foods has been woven from similar threads. Consider the mid-20th-century dinner party classic known as Texas caviar, a spicy salad of black-eyed peas, onion, garlic, peppers, cilantro, and oil and vinegar. Texas caviar was the creation of the great chef and tastemaker Helen Corbitt, who cooked in some of the state's finest hotels, clubs, and restaurants, including the one on the top floor of the flagship Neiman Marcus store in Dallas (see page 94). In 1940, Corbitt, who'd just moved to Austin from New York City, was asked to

IN 2011, *BON APPÉTIT* DECLARED AUSTIN'S FRANKLIN BARBECUE THE "BEST BBQ RESTAURANT IN AMERICA."

cater a fancy dinner. Unable to find caviar and other luxury ingredients she was familiar with, she turned to Texas's local larder, namely the tasty little legumes known as black-eyed peas. Texas caviar was born.

Look at the history of almost any iconic Texas food and similar stories emerge. Hill Country barbecue? Tip your hat to German- and Czech-born butchers who employed old-world smoking methods to preserve leftover meat. Cowboy-style chili? You can thank Texas frontiersmen who used hot peppers and suet to bring dried beef back to life. Even mass-market snack foods from Texas have

thrifty origins. The Frito was the brainchild of a San Antonio resident named Charles Elmer Doolin, who came up with his idea in 1932 while crunching on leftover corn tortillas that had been deep-fried and served with his lunch at a local restaurant. Like a lot of Texas food firsts, his went on to become as American as apple pie.

Opposite: Domesticity on wheels at a migrant camp in Harlingen, in 1939, where resourceful Texans attached kitchen cabinets to two-wheeled trailers. This page, clockwise from top left: Dinner patrons at Rock Cafe; chicken-fried steak, anyone?; none for this couple, who spiced things up at a chili cook-off in Terlingua; sometimes the best barbecue comes from galvanized metal stands, such as this one in Corpus Christi.

COMMONSENSE TAXATION

There's nothing like a side-by-side comparison of taxes and regulations in California and Texas to show just how badly California is getting it wrong these days. As a whole, Californians spend 46 percent more of their income on government fees and taxes than Texans do. More than two hundred government departments in California are proposing an average of seven hundred regulatory packages a year, each package containing as many as thirty new regulations. According to a 2009 study, those regulations—including overtime laws that are onerous to employers wanting to give greater work-day flexibility to employees—cost California small businesses almost $493 billion and cost the state some 3.8 million jobs. California also has one of the highest franchise tax rates in the country (a franchise tax is a fee required by the government for a company to do business in a state); Texas has one of the lowest. A fledgling company in Texas with small revenues won't pay any franchise tax at all.

A Regulation Report Card, Based on a Survey of 6,000 Small Business Owners

CALIFORNIA	
Overall regulatory friendliness	F
Friendliness of health and safety regulations	F
Friendliness of employment, labor, and hiring regulations	F
Friendliness of tax code	F
Friendliness of licensing regulations	F
Friendliness of environmental regulations	F
Friendliness of zoning regulations	D

TEXAS	
Overall regulatory friendliness	A
Friendliness of health and safety regulations	A-
Friendliness of employment, labor, and hiring regulations	A
Friendliness of tax code	A
Friendliness of licensing regulations	A
Friendliness of environmental regulations	A-
Friendliness of zoning regulations	A

AND REGULATION

Franchise Tax Rates in Texas and California

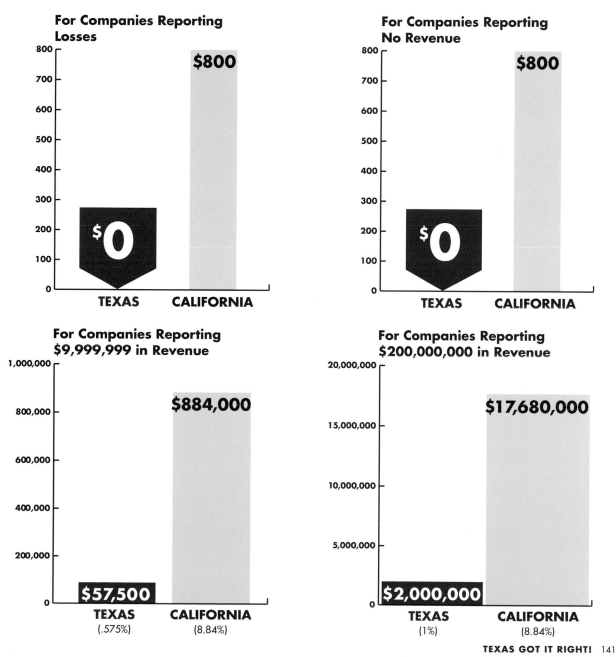

For Companies Reporting Losses

	TEXAS	CALIFORNIA
	$0	$800

For Companies Reporting No Revenue

	TEXAS	CALIFORNIA
	$0	$800

For Companies Reporting $9,999,999 in Revenue

	TEXAS (.575%)	CALIFORNIA (8.84%)
	$57,500	$884,000

For Companies Reporting $200,000,000 in Revenue

	TEXAS (1%)	CALIFORNIA (8.84%)
	$2,000,000	$17,680,000

A DOLLAR GOES FURTHER
IN TEXAS

You get more for your money in the Lone Star State—more space to live and sleep, more food, more services, more daily necessities, more of almost anything. Texas has one of the most attractive cost-of-living indices in the country, owing to a happy confluence of cheap energy, ample housing stock, well-developed

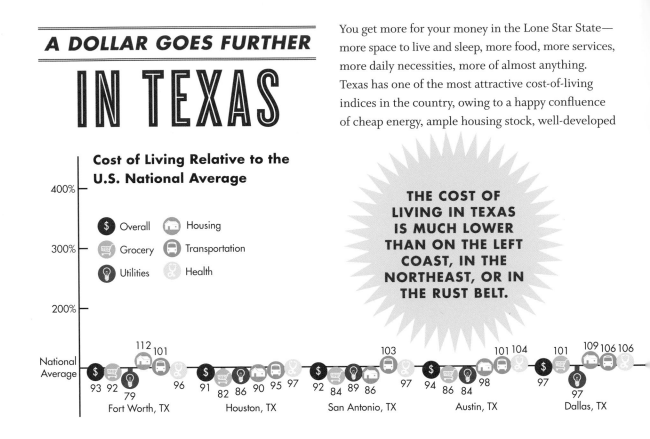

Cost of Living Relative to the U.S. National Average

$ Overall   🏠 Housing
🛒 Grocery   🚌 Transportation
💡 Utilities   ⚕ Health

THE COST OF LIVING IN TEXAS IS MUCH LOWER THAN ON THE LEFT COAST, IN THE NORTHEAST, OR IN THE RUST BELT.

Fort Worth, TX: 93, 92, 79, 112, 101, 96

Houston, TX: 91, 82, 86, 90, 95, 97

San Antonio, TX: 92, 84, 89, 86, 103, 97

Austin, TX: 94, 86, 84, 98, 101, 104

Dallas, TX: 97, 97, 109, 106, 106, 101

Fill Your Tank for Less in Texas

Range (in miles) on $50 of Gas

Fort Worth, TX	$50 Buys 14.5 Gallons of Gas	**291 Miles**
San Antonio, TX	$50 Buys 14.5 Gallons of Gas	**291 Miles**
Dallas, TX	$50 Buys 14.5 Gallons of Gas	**291 Miles**
Austin, TX	$50 Buys 14.3 Gallons of Gas	**285 Miles**
Houston, TX	$50 Buys 14.2 Gallons of Gas	**283 Miles**
Boston, MA	$50 Buys 13.6 Gallons of Gas	**271 Miles**
Philadelphia, PA	$50 Buys 13.3 Gallons of Gas	**265 Miles**
New York, NY	$50 Buys 12.5 Gallons of Gas	**250 Miles**
Chicago, IL	$50 Buys 11.7 Gallons of Gas	**235 Miles**
Los Angeles, CA	$50 Buys 11.6 Gallons of Gas	**231 Miles**

0   50   100   150   200   250   300

transportation networks, an extensive agriculture sector, low taxes, and less bureaucracy, among other factors. Even in its thriving and increasingly affluent big cities, where the pressures of population density increase demand for goods and housing, basic expenditures like rent and groceries are only slightly above the national average—a far cry from notoriously pricey cities like New York and San Francisco. What's more, urban centers in Texas that are enjoying record job growth and growing cosmopolitan cachet are still comparatively cheaper places to live than economically struggling cities like Chicago and Los Angeles.

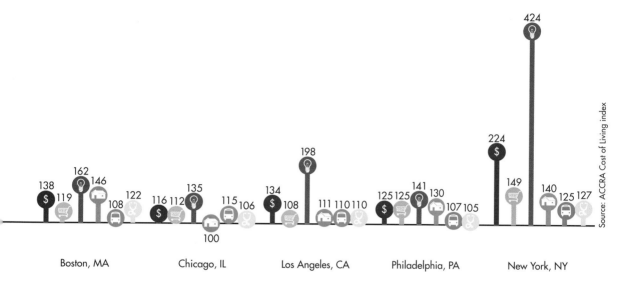

Source: ACCRA Cost of Living index

Boston, MA Chicago, IL Los Angeles, CA Philadelphia, PA New York, NY

⬤ Most Expensive Cities

1 New York (Manhattan), NY
2 New York (Brooklyn), NY
3 Honolulu, HI
4 San Francisco, CA
5 New York (Queens), NY
6 San Jose, CA
7 Stamford, CT
8 Truckee-Nevada County, CA
9 Washington, DC
10 Orange County, CA

⬤ Least Expensive Cities

1 Harlingen, TX
2 Pueblo, CO
3 McAllen, TX
4 Temple, TX
5 Memphis, TN
6 Cookeville, TN
7 Richmond, IN
8 Waco, TX
9 Ardmore, OK
10 Sherman-Denison, TX

A HOUSING MARKET
OPEN TO ALL

**Average Square Footage
of a $250,000 Home**

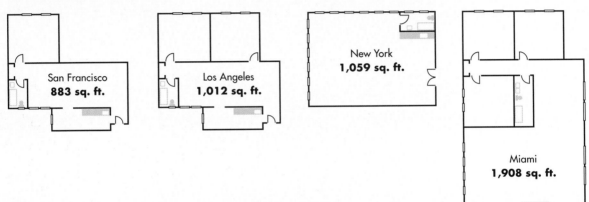

San Francisco
883 sq. ft.

Los Angeles
1,012 sq. ft.

New York
1,059 sq. ft.

Miami
1,908 sq. ft.

**Cost Per Ton
of Garbage**

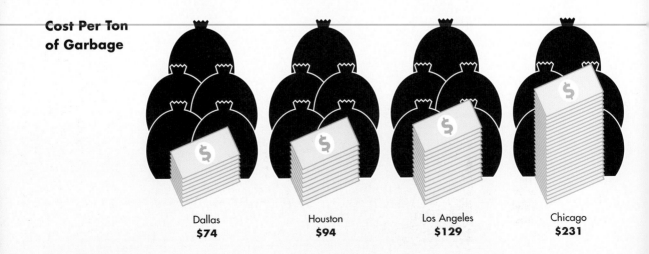

Dallas
$74

Houston
$94

Los Angeles
$129

Chicago
$231

Coastal U.S. cities, with their limited housing stock and no-growth zoning laws, are becoming less and less accessible to middle-class working families and young college grads—even as nearby inland communities are being gutted by overbuilding and foreclosures. Texas has steered clear of both extremes. The Lone Star State led the country in building permits in 2011 and—thanks to stricter lending laws, among other factors—largely escaped both the housing bubble and its aftermath, having emerged from the Great Recession with a foreclosure rate that's roughly half the national average. Add to those factors another advantage: You get a lot more for your housing dollar in Texas. That's true even in our biggest cities, and it means that fewer families are spending a precarious percentage of their income on housing. (California leads the nation in that dubious honor.) All this is not just because Texas cities have room to grow—though they have plenty of that. It's also because local governments in Texas are leaner than those of patronage-plagued cities like Chicago, a fact that allows our municipalities to charge less for basic services.

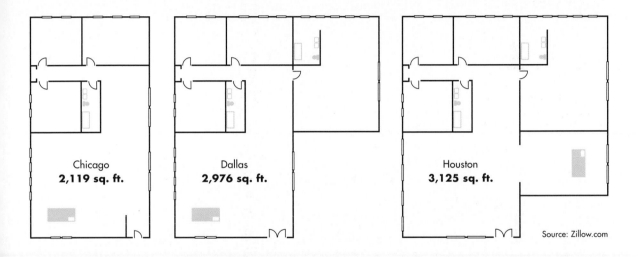

Chicago
2,119 sq. ft.

Dallas
2,976 sq. ft.

Houston
3,125 sq. ft.

Source: Zillow.com

Percentage of Working Households Spending More Than 50% of Income on Housing

San Antonio 17%

Dallas 21%

New York 34%

Los Angeles 38%

Miami 43%

WE GOT
ROOM TO ROAM

Wide-open spaces are what drew the earliest European settlers to Texas, and the sheer vastness of the Lone Star State remains perhaps its most cherished asset. The High Plains in the north, the great pine forests in the east, the high desert in the west, the sprawling rangelands in the south, the otherworldly beauty of Big Bend, the splendor of the Rio Grande Valley—these are landscapes that awaken towering ambitions and big dreams.

TEXAS GAME-CHANGER
SOUTHWEST AIRLINES

Want to avoid the death grip of Washington regulators and get a little entrepreneurial inspiration while you're at it? Just follow in the footsteps of Southwest Airlines. According to cofounder Herb Kelleher, who is credited with creating one of the most successful corporate cultures in the country, the idea for the company was born on a cocktail napkin sometime around 1970. Southwest Airlines was born a year later, with just a handful of employees and a nearly nonexistent fleet.

"The very first Sunday morning of Southwest's life," recalls Kelleher's colleague Lamar Muse in his book *Southwest Passage*, "we narrowly escaped a disaster. During the takeoff run, the right thrust-reverser deployed. Only the captain's instantaneous reaction allowed him to recover control and make a tight turn for an emergency landing on one engine." But the kinks got worked out, and soon Kelleher and his team were writing the book on running a no-frills, low-cost airline that knew how to keep both leisure and business flyers happy.

Truth be told, Southwest owed a good measure of its success to Texas itself. The state, it turned out, was a good place to start an airline from scratch. In the early 1970s, interstate airlines were controlled by the Civil Aeronautics Board, which was notoriously slow to approve new carriers and even slower to assign routes. By keeping its business inside Texas at first—a perfectly viable option given the state's immense size—Southwest just had to cajole a certificate of operation from the Texas Aeronautics Commission. Sure, the airline clashed in court with local competitors Braniff and Texas International, but it won the right to fly. And when the industry was deregulated in 1979, Southwest had enough cash and clout to make it outside the Lone Star State.

Southwest was an early adopter of the Boeing 737 jet—a bold move at a time when older turboprops like the Lockheed Electra were considered standard for regional carriers. There were logistical leaps as well. Early on, Muse made the decision to base the airline at smaller, close-to-downtown airports—Hobby in Houston and Love Field in Dallas—as a boon to business travelers. Southwest also inaugurated the practice of offering ridiculously low fares—$20 each way between Dallas, Houston, and San Antonio in the early days. For its main routes to and from Dallas, Southwest soon started offering $13 bargain-traveler fares on nights and weekends. Seat occupancy doubled in less than a month. Soon Southwest had changed the whole landscape of aviation in Texas and surrounding states. Braniff—the region's big legacy airline—went bust in the face of this newly focused competitor, and lots of folks who had flown their own planes to dozens of hard-to-get-to Texas towns now saw that they could fly Southwest for a whole lot cheaper.

Kelleher and his colleagues had a peculiarly Texan knack for pleasing the average traveler. Among other things, they introduced hot pants–clad "air hostesses." And as a hedge against the competition, Southwest started throwing in a free bottle of premium liquor with the purchase of every full-fare $26 ticket. Business travelers flying on expense accounts flocked to Southwest, buying the more expensive ticket and keeping the booze.

Opposite: Herb Kelleher covers his ears as a Southwest jet taxis to the runway on Love Field in 1985. This page, clockwise from top left: Southwest Airlines stewardesses put their best boots forward, circa 1968; they justified the company's billboard slogans; Lamar Muse in 1981; in 2010, Southwest bought rival AirTran, a move that brought the company's distinctive orange and blue jets to dozens of new cities.

NOBODY MESSES WITH
THE TEXAS RANGERS

Fifty years ago, the city of Dallas dedicated a bronze statue of a Texas Ranger at Love Field airport. It's just a man with a cowboy hat, boots, and a holstered pistol, plus a brief inscription: "One riot. One Ranger!" More on the riot in a minute, but about those Texas Rangers: Formed by order of Empresario Stephen Austin in 1823 to protect Texan settlers, this all-volunteer law-enforcement unit is the original Delta Force, the very definition of an elite, highly mobile expeditionary team. These are the guys who captured the outlaw John Wesley Hardin and ended the bank-robbing career of Sam Bass. They battled Comanches at Palo Duro Canyon and fought Yankees during the Civil War. In the 1930s, when the above photograph was taken, a few Rangers of the day gunned down Bonnie and Clyde near Ruston, Louisiana, after tracking them across nine states.

As for that riot? Well, when the East Texas oil fields blew in 1930, attracting a rush of wildcatters, roughnecks, roustabouts, and all manner of riffraff, the local sheriff and his deputies couldn't contain the mayhem. So he called for a detachment of Texas Rangers. When he met the train that was supposed to be carrying them, only one Ranger got off. "Where's all the Rangers?" the sheriff asked. The lone Ranger answered: "You got one riot. You got one Ranger!"

Opposite: Preparing for the Texas Centennial Exposition in 1936, a group of Texas Rangers check out the replica frontier house that will host their exhibit. This page, top: Formed by well-to-do planter Benjamin Franklin Terry in 1861, the Eighth Texas Cavalry Regiment, or Terry's Texas Rangers, fought valiantly for the Confederates during the Civil War. Middle: A monument to Terry's unit stands at the Texas Capitol. Bottom: Texas Rangers spared no ammo when they finally caught up with Bonnie and Clyde.

That's what's so deeply Texan about the Rangers: They are problem solvers, trained to git 'er done with minimal resources. That could mean surviving on wild game and wearing coats made from animal skins, as they did in the 1800s, or quelling a riot with a man and a pistol. "A Ranger can handle any given situation without definite instructions from [a] higher authority," said Bob Crowder, a Ranger captain in the 1950s and '60s who once strode into a hostage siege at a hospital by himself, *wearing his gun.* He calmly talked the eighty-one armed inmates into putting down their weapons without ever drawing his. Not a bullet or a life wasted—resourceful and courageous to the core.

TEXANS TOOK FOOTBALL TO THE NEXT LEVEL

The first Super Bowl may have been played in Los Angeles, but the idea came from a Texan, Lamar Hunt, the sixth child of oil man H. L. Hunt (known in the 1950s as "the richest man in the world") and a third-team bench warmer on the SMU football team. Lamar proved to be one of the shrewdest minds in the history of pro sports. In 1959, NFL commissioner Bert Bell rebuffed Hunt's proposal to expand the league in order to bring pro football to Dallas. The twelve-team NFL wasn't interested in any city south of St. Louis. So, like a good Texas entrepreneur, Hunt decided to start his own league. His American Football League would eventually field ten teams, recruit some of the most legendary players of the era, and compete successfully with the old NFL. Pro football got to cities that had been deprived of a team—like Dallas, Houston, New Orleans, and Atlanta—and Lamar's league helped break the color barrier by recruiting heavily from black colleges like Grambling, in Louisiana.

In 1966, after TV money had gotten bigger and Hunt's AFL had become a formidable competitor for the Rust Belt teams of the North and Northeast, a delegation of National Football League guys approached Hunt and proposed merger talks in order to re-establish a quasinational monopoly, protected by an exemption to federal antitrust laws. All the Hunt league teams were absorbed into the new monster intact. In 1970 they would morph into two conferences and would play a title game at the end of the season. Hunt, after seeing his kids playing with a Super Ball, dubbed the matchup "the Super Bowl."

Above: In 1960, when the Cowboys were formed, defensive tackle Bob Lilly (#74) became coach Tom Landry's first draft pick. Inset: In his trademark fedora, Landry led America's team for twenty-nine seasons, racking up 270 wins.

Lamar Hunt fundamentally altered the business of
pro football (see opposite page), Tom Landry and
Tex Schramm redefined the game itself—and the
way we watch it. During their twenty-nine-season
tenure as coach and general manager of the Dallas
Cowboys, these Texans introduced instant replay,
computer-driven scouting, and the thirty-second
play clock, among other innovations. And, in a
stroke of theatrical brilliance,
Schramm gave us the modern-day
Dallas Cowboy Cheerleaders. In
1972 he scrapped the conventional
lineup of pom-pom-waving, slogan-
chanting high school students in
favor of a chorus line of profession-
ally trained and provocatively clad
dancers. When the new and
improved cheerleader squad—fresh
from a summer training camp run
by Dallas dance studio owner Texie

Waterman—made their debut in spangles and knee
boots at Texas Stadium in 1972, it was literally a
whole new ball game. Schramm saw pro football not
only as a sport, but also as a televised spectacle.
Today, the Dallas Cowboys are called "America's
Team" and are the highest-valued sports franchise in
the United States, in no small part thanks to
Schramm and a Dallas dance teacher.

...AND TURNED

CHEERLEADERS

INTO

SUPERSTARS

By 1979, the new-and-improved Dallas
Cowboy Cheerleaders had become

OUR SMALL TOWN HEROES
WEAR CLEATS

Nowhere is the religion of Texas high school football more alive than in a "six-man town." They've got names like Zephyr, Whitharral, Paint Rock, Panther Creek, Penelope, Star, and Spur: rural communities too small to field a standard eleven-man high school team. For them, six-man football—first played in Texas in the 1930s—is a godsend. There are currently 183 state-sanctioned six-man teams in Texas; that number doesn't include private-school squads or the dozens of "outlaw" teams fielded by high schools that have enough students for eleven-man football but play six-man anyhow.

Pay a visit to virtually any six-man town in Texas on an autumn Friday night and you'll see why the game is so popular. Played on an eighty-yard field under rules that allow any player to be a receiver, six-man is a blazing-fast, high-scoring game. "[N]othing can match six-man's speed and excitement, where teams often combine for more than one hundred points in a game," wrote the great Cowboys quarterback Troy Aikman in his foreword for Laura Wilson's *Grit and Glory*. A selection of photographs from Wilson's book, which documents six-man across small-town Texas, is pictured here. "In six-man, anything can happen." The players are as tough and dedicated as any of their eleven-man-team counterparts, some more so. For them, and for the fans who cheer them on at little 150-plus-seat stadiums all over rural Texas, six-man is the ultimate display of hometown pride.

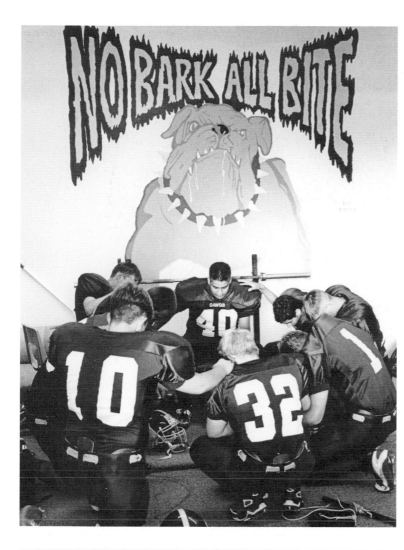

"When I like something, I never just want one picture; I always want more," says Laura Wilson of her photographs. "Many of the playing fields were crudely lit. I had to be close to the action to get any picture at all. In retrospect, my style fit the sport—direct and pared down. My approach didn't depend on the latest breakthrough equipment; it depended on the atmosphere of those Friday nights, the thrill of the action and my own sense of story ... The memories of the towns, the boys, the coaches—the whole ethos of six-man football—will always stick with me. And I'll look for six-man scores in the newspaper on fall Saturday mornings."

WE GROW UP TO BE
DAREDEVILS & BRONC RIDERS

From the statehouse (see page 40) to the U.S. Senate (page 38) to the executive suite (page 160), the Lone Star State has been built on the shoulders of tough, determined, charismatic women. What other state could have produced the likes of Bessie Coleman, the daughter of a poor sharecropper who would go on to become the first black licensed airplane pilot in history and one of aviation's most legendary daredevils? Where else could a group of cowgirls coming of age just after the war have gotten together and said, "Let's start our own rodeo!" That's what the women of the Girls' Rodeo Association did in San Angelo, Texas, in 1948.

Today their group, now called the Women's Professional Rodeo Association, hosts competitive events all over the country and is the oldest women's professional sports organization in America, and the only one governed entirely by women. What motivated them is the same thing that motivates any Texan to achieve great things. It's a simple matter of saying to yourself, "This is what I'm good at, and I'm gonna do it better than anyone else."

Above: Coleman, circa 1920. Opposite: Before the bull riding and the calf roping at a rodeo comes the parade, always led by beautiful horses, beautiful girls (some who can actually break a bronco), and American flags.

SANDRA DAY O'CONNOR WAS THE 2002 COWGIRL HONOREE OF FORT WORTH'S NATIONAL COWGIRL MUSEUM.

TEXAS LOVES A MAN OR WOMAN
IN A UNIFORM

To say that Texas is military-friendly doesn't quite express just how important the armed forces are to the everyday life of hundreds of thousands of Texans. That's been the case since the 19th century, when the U.S. government established forts and garrisons ever deeper in Texas territory to pave the way for the nation's westward expansion. Today, Texas is home to nearly 200,000 active-duty members of the military, spread across eight air force bases, two naval air stations, and five army bases, including the largest one in the country, Fort Hood. That base alone saw 300,000 military deployments during the Iraq War and suffered the war's greatest losses: some five hundred men and women killed in action, more than any other military installation in the country. Soldiers from Fort Hood were among the last regular units to leave Iraq during the conflict's final months, and commanders from that base ran the day-to-day operations of the war for half its duration.

While national military budgets are shrinking, Texas's commitment is expanding. Dyess Air Force Base, just outside Abilene, puts 5,000 people to work, making it the largest employer in the area. Other big bases, from El Paso's Fort Bliss to the Corpus Christi Naval Air Station, play similarly important roles in local economies.

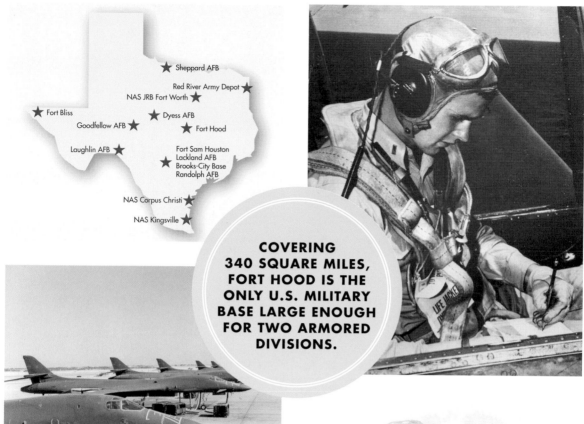

Sheppard AFB
Red River Army Depot
NAS JRB Fort Worth
Fort Bliss
Goodfellow AFB
Dyess AFB
Fort Hood
Laughlin AFB
Fort Sam Houston
Lackland AFB
Brooks-City Base
Randolph AFB
NAS Corpus Christi
NAS Kingsville

COVERING 340 SQUARE MILES, FORT HOOD IS THE ONLY U.S. MILITARY BASE LARGE ENOUGH FOR TWO ARMORED DIVISIONS.

In 2003 Dyess AFB became the first base in the United States to be powered exclusively by renewable wind energy, making it a proving ground for a lot more than just bombers and fighters.

Opposite: In March 2008, Spc. Monica Lin Brown of Lake Jackson became the fifth female solider since World War II to win the Silver Star. This page, clockwise from top left: a map of Texas military bases; President George H.W. Bush—who was the youngest pilot in the navy when he earned his wings at Corpus Christi Naval Air Station—in his TBM Avenger torpedo bomber on the USS San Jacinto, 1944; Sgt. Howard Acoff hugs his family as U.S. Army 1st Cavalry 3rd Brigade soldiers return home from Iraq on Christmas Eve at Fort Hood, Texas, 2011; B1-B bombers ready for action at Dyess Air Force Base, 1987.

TEXAS GAME-CHANGER
MARY KAY ASH

Decades before Oprah Winfrey had the idea, a visionary Texan named Mary Kay Ash had discovered the value of giving away brand-new cars—and we're not talking about a Pontiac G6.

Ash, the Texas-born founder of Mary Kay cosmetics, didn't believe in cash bonuses, but she did believe in Pink Cadillacs, which she offered as an incentive to her best saleswomen. She called the cars "rolling trophies," in keeping with her notion that success should be rewarded conspicuously and that femininity should be flaunted. It goes without saying that she drove a Pink Caddy herself. The car's paint job was a custom hue based on the color of a Mary Kay cosmetics case. "They painted it that delicate shade of pink and it became a sensation in Dallas," she was quoted as saying in a 1985 *Washington Post* article. "You drive up to an intersection, and I don't care if the traffic is going in eight directions, they stop and let you through. The waters part."

If Mary Kay Ash was a woman for whom waters parted, it was not the result of privilege or luck. She worked her way into that plush driver's seat. For twenty-five years she worked in direct sales, rising to the job of national training director at the World Gift Company. But when a man she had trained was promoted to the job of her supervisor and paid twice as much as she was getting, Ash decided to quit and write a book.

That book became a business plan, and in 1963, at the age of forty-five, Ash started her namesake company. Her son, Richard Rogers, became her partner (and would go on to shepherd the company to ever greater successes). She staffed the Dallas office with nine saleswomen, called independent beauty consultants, and hit the road to drum up customers. Mary Kay cosmetics' first big success was a skin softener. By the end of the company's first year of operation, it had generated $200,000 in sales. That jumped to $800,000 the following year.

Members of Mary Kay's sales force were encouraged by Ash to put "God first, family second, and career third." They set their own schedules and built their own customer base, meaning that if they chose to bump career up a notch in that holy trinity, that was their prerogative. Plus, Ash put in place a system of incentives—from mink coats and vacation trips to those Pink Cadillacs—that fostered go-getters. Achieving one of the exalted national sales director positions at Mary Kay could mean an income of hundreds of thousands of dollars a year. Mary Kay cosmetics may have produced more wealthy women than any other company in America.

"I am working for the economic liberation of women," Ash said. Then, as if to answer the growing chorus of feminists who considered her approach to liberation more than a little regressive and outré, she added, "But I think God knew what he was doing when he made men and women, and I think we're supposed to remain female." For Ash, who favored magnificent bouffants and patrician jewelry,

self-denial and false modesty just weren't part of the program. The cosmetics seminar Ash held in Dallas every year attracted thousands of sales reps, each of whom paid their own way to hear, cheer, and revere their founder. "You would have thought I was their long-lost mother," she observed. "Because I am their long-lost mother. Because that's the attitude that I take toward any one of them, whatever they may need or whatever I can do to help them."

Throughout her life, Ash accumulated a veritable catalog of pithy sayings, such as: "If a woman feels pretty on the outside, she becomes prettier on the inside, too," and, "You can't rest on your laurels, for nothing wilts faster than a laurel rested upon." But her flair for phrase-making was merely a footnote to her more tangible legacy: a business that today employs 2 million people in thirty-seven countries and has annual wholesale sales in the multibillions. That's a lot of pink makeup cases.

MICHIGAN SALESMAN JIM CUNDIFF WAS THE FIRST MAN TO WIN A MARY KAY CADILLAC.

Opposite: Mary Kay Ash holds her Horatio Alger Award, 1978. This page, left: Robin Tucker (front) and other Mary Kay independent beauty consultants show off their pink Cadillacs while making a video for their fortieth-anniversary convention in front of Dallas City Hall. Right: During her twenty-eight years as a Mary Kay salesperson and director, Sarabel Epperson of Dallas has won more than twelve pink Cadillacs.

TEXANS ARE GREAT AT
DOING GOOD

If you want to see the future of nonprofit advocacy in America, go to Dallas. It's home to the headquarters of Susan G. Komen for the Cure, the breast-cancer charity founded by Nancy Brinker in 1982, two years after her sister Susan lost her battle to the disease. In 2012, Komen for the Cure had 124 branch offices around the world and 216 corporate partnerships and had organized 130 Race for the Cure events, which in many cities have become as much a part of the cultural landscape as a Fourth of July parade. The foundation's pink ribbon is one of the most potent brand icons in the country, a shining example of how corporate marketing strategies can achieve extraordinary results in a nonprofit context.

Brinker was born in Peoria, Illinois, and moved to Dallas in 1968 to work at Neiman Marcus, the specialty store chain that rewrote the book on the art of the sale (see page 94). Dallas turned out to be the best place she could have possibly chosen for her future life's mission. Philanthropy is part of the fabric of everyday life in the city—with charity events figuring as prominently on social calendars as Friday-night football. The city's skyline is dotted with buildings bearing the names of prominent Texans—from the Wyly Theater downtown to the Hamon Tower at Texas Presbyterian Hospital—who have prospered in

BY 2012, THE KOMEN FOUNDATION HAD INVESTED MORE THAN $1.9 BILLION IN THE FIGHT AGAINST BREAST CANCER.

the Lone Star State and have given as good as they got. So when Brinker decided she needed to make a difference in the fight against breast cancer after her sister passed away in 1980, she approached the successful Dallas restaurant-chain entrepreneur Norman Brinker, whose first wife had died of ovarian cancer in her thirties. Norman and Nancy got married in 1981, and the first Race for the Cure was held in Dallas two years later. It drew 800 runners. Today, some 1.6 million people run every year.

Scores of other globally influential nonprofits thrive in Texas, from the Livestrong Foundation in Austin—creator of the yellow plastic wristband that

has conquered the world—to the Dallas-headquartered American Heart Association, which gets more than $500 million from private donors every year.

It's simple, really. The things that make Texans so good at making money in business are the same things that make them great at raising it for a cause.

Left: Komen founder Nancy Brinker (with umbrella) greets young supporters at a 2007 rally in Washington, D.C. Above, clockwise from top left: Members of the Race for the Cure prepare the stage in front of the Washington Monument in June of 2000; participant Jennifer Davis carries a sign during a 2011 Race for the Cure event in Detroit; sixty-seven-year-old Adba Carollamb gets her groove on at the twentieth annual Race for the Cure in Detroit.

TORT REFORM — A BIG WIN

Before Governor Rick Perry's landmark 2003 tort-reform legislation, one out of every four doctors in Texas had a malpractice claim filed against him or her in any given year. Eighty-six percent of those cases resulted in no payment to the plaintiff, but that didn't stop medical liability-insurance premiums from soaring, or prevent doctors from fleeing the state (even as Texas's population was growing). The 2003 reforms—which, among other things, cap pain-and-suffering awards and require the loser of a case deemed bogus by the court to pay all legal fees—turned things around virtually overnight. Thousands

Number of Physicians in Texas, 2011

} Practices Established After 2003 Tort Reform (Approx. 5,000)

51,217 Total

Texas Medical Liability-Insurance Premiums

Before 2003 Tort Reform

After 2003 Tort Reform (46.24% decrease)

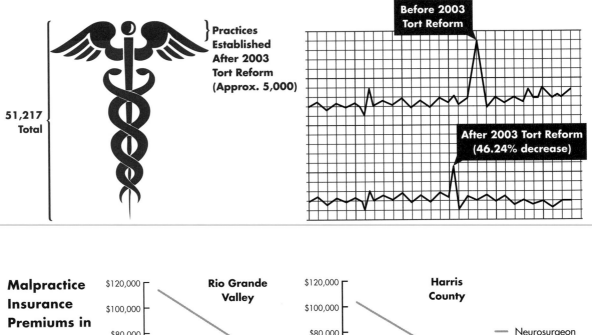

Malpractice Insurance Premiums in Two Texas Markets

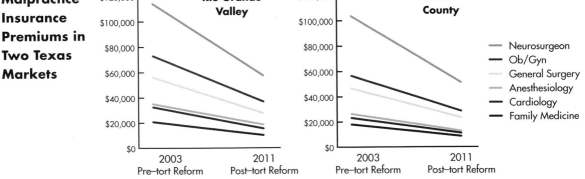

Rio Grande Valley

Harris County

- Neurosurgeon
- Ob/Gyn
- General Surgery
- Anesthesiology
- Cardiology
- Family Medicine

FOR DOCTORS AND PATIENTS

of doctors have established new practices in Texas since 2003, many of them in previously underserved counties. The Texas Medical Board received 83 percent more applications in the four years after the reform than in the four years preceding it. The vast majority of those doctors cited Texas's superior "liability climate" as a primary reason for their move, according to a survey by the Texas Medical Association. Moreover, the cost of liability insurance has dropped dramatically, as has the cost to consumers, who had to foot the bill for malpractice litigation in the form of higher-priced goods and services.

Texas Counties That Got Their First ER Doctor After 2003 Reform

TEXAS GAME-CHANGER
RICHARD FISHER

"When I was sworn into office, I checked all politics and partisanship at the door. I am neither an 'R' nor a 'D'; I am politically indifferent. When I took this job, Alan Greenspan told me I had only one obligation, which in his words was 'to speak to the truth.' I do my best to speak the straight skinny, informed by the work of the staff of the Dallas Fed, the input I receive from the bankers and businesses and citizens of my district, and my own career as a banker, an investor, a trade negotiator, and a man smart enough to come to Texas thirty-seven years ago."

—Richard Fisher, Austin, 2010

Most Americans have never heard of him. Heck, most Texans probably haven't either. But if there's one guy who embodies everything that's right about the way we're doing business in Texas today, it's Richard Fisher.

Fisher is not an oilman or a rancher or a hotshot start-up CEO. He wears sober-looking suits to work, is graying around the temples, and has a résumé that hardly reads like a maverick's: college at the U.S. Naval Academy and Harvard, graduate work at Oxford, MBA from Stanford, a stint at a New York investment bank, then a senior Treasury position under the Carter administration followed by a series of high-level federal jobs and now president and chief executive of the Federal Reserve Bank of Dallas.

But if Texas entrepreneurs ever wanted a good man on the inside, they've got one in Richard Fisher. As a member of the Federal Open Market Committee, the Federal Reserve's main fiscal policy-making group, Fisher has earned a reputation for speaking "the straight skinny" (to borrow his own words) and has frequently cast dissenting votes as one of the seventeen who compose the FOMC. He was an outspoken voice against the group's decisions to push down longer-term interest rates, believing that, as he said, the Fed can provide the fuel but small banks and businesses have to put their foot on the gas.

During a speech in 2010 to the Economic Club of Minnesota, Fisher expressed profound misgivings about the Fed's fiscal policy, pointing out that many of the large corporations he'd recently surveyed were committing themselves to deploying cheap money abroad, where taxes were lower and governments were more eager to please. "I believe what is restraining our economy is not monetary policy but fiscal misfeasance in Washington," he said. The straight skinny indeed.

Fisher frequently holds Texas up as a model for economic growth for the rest of the country. The state "has a long tradition of outperforming the nation," and Texans, he added, "don't linger long on the old, and we are quick to usher in the new." As he saw it, the key to Lone Star success was the ability to adapt quickly in a globalized and competitive eco-

nomic landscape. "Texas's transition from a resource-based economy built on cattle, cotton, and oil to a knowledge-based economy built on human capital and innovation is our greatest success," he said. "We have made a fine transition from cow chips to computer chips and from boots to suits."

In short, Fisher believes that Texas works better because of its low tax and regulatory burdens, flexible labor markets, open land availability, tort reform, great seaports and airports, and robust communication infrastructure. To all of which we say: *exactly*.

Fisher is an apolitical animal—"I am neither an 'R' nor a 'D,'" he's said—and was appointed not by the president but by the directors of the Dallas Federal Reserve Bank's board, which is made up of feet-on-the-ground businessmen from the Fed's Eleventh District, which is mostly Texas. This here's an entrepreneur's policymaker if ever there was one.

Opposite: Serving as a deputy U.S. trade representative, Fisher fields questions in March 2000 after failing to reach an agreement with Japan over the deregulation of that country's telecommunications industry. This page: During remarks before the Texas Manufacturers Summit in 2012, Fisher used these charts to show how Texas continues to outperform the nation—and the world—in economic growth and job expansion.

Job Growth Around the Globe

Job growth index, 100 = January 1990.
(except Euro Area, where 100 = July 1990)

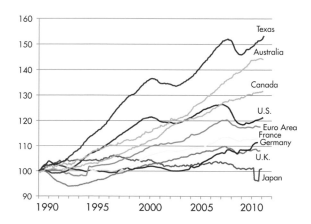

Total Nonagricultural Employment in Selected States Since 1990

Job growth index, 100 = January 1990

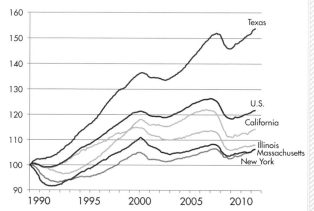

LIGHTEN THE BURDEN

Abolish the state income tax and scale franchise taxes to favor the quick growth of new and emerging businesses.

STREAMLINE THE STATEHOUSE

Limit state legislators' pay and reduce the number of days per year they meet. Lawmakers who have to earn a living in the real world pass commonsense laws!

HOW TO BE MORE LIKE TEXAS... IN TEN EASY STEPS

An at-a-glance policy guide to emulating the business-friendliest state in America

SAY NO TO FENCES

Encourage cross-border trade and legal immigration. They are an economic boon for border states, not a threat.

CUT THE RED TAPE

Pass commonsense zoning laws—when you have to pass them at all—and streamline the permitting process for commercial and residential development.

DEREGULATE... FOR REAL

Create a truly competitive consumer market-place for utilities in order to bring down prices and attract clean-energy companies. And we don't mean Lenin-style state-managed deregulation, like in California; we mean Adam Smith–style, like in Texas!

OPEN UP THE SHOP

Pass right-to-work laws that protect employees from mandatory union member-ship—and keep companies' doors wide open to hiring.

FRACK WITH LOVING CARE

Clear the way for responsible hydraulic fracturing, horizontal drilling, and other proven natural-gas extraction techniques, and keep our country on the path to clean power and energy independence.

SEND THE AMBULANCE CHASERS PACKING

Enact medical-malpractice tort reform, which limits damages and deters frivolous lawsuits, and is the best way to attract new doctors and improve coverage for everyone.

STAND BY THE HOMESTEADER

Honor the spirit of the Texas Homestead Act—and say good-bye to housing bubbles—by establishing strong safeguards against irresponsible lending, runaway real estate speculation, and predatory foreclosure practices.

CHOOSE WISELY; IT'S A SMALL PLANET!

Promote economic development that respects the environment. Texas has proven that con-servation and growth can go hand in hand.

INDEX

Note: Italic page numbers refer to infographics and illustrations.

CREDITS

IMAGE CREDITS:

All infographic elements designed by Naomi Mizusaki unless otherwise credited.

Front cover (illustration): GuiTAJ/vectorstock.com; 3 (illustration): GuiTAJ/vectorstock.com; 10: Courtesy of the Wyly family; 13: Courtesy of the Wyly family; 16: David Wright/Courtesy of the Wyly family; 19: Bob Stefko; 21: Paul Gaither; 22 (painting): Charles Shaw, (flag): Encyclopedia Britannica/UIF; 23 (flag): Visions of America/Joe Sohn; 26: Southern Methodist University/Central University Libraries/DeGolyer Library; 27 (monument): James Pharaon; 28: based on a map in Colin Woodward's *American Nations*; 29: Gillespie County Historical Society; 30: Associated Press; 31 (top): Visions of America/Joe Sohn, (bottom): Publishing Resources/Charles Edwards; 32: Lucchese Boot Company; 33 (clockwise from top left): Lucchese Boot Company, Ellen Appell, Lucchese Boot Company; 34: AP Photo/Henry Burroughs; 35: AP Photo/File; 36: Yoichi R. Okamoto/Lyndon Baines Johnson Library and Museum; 37: Clint Grant/Dallas Morning News; 38: Texas State Library & Archives Commission; 39: Reuters/Mike Stone; 40: (Mark Homer): Courtesy of *The Texas Tribune*, (Robert Nichols): Courtesy of the Senate of Texas, (all other images): Courtesy of the Texas House of Representatives; 44 (top): 7-11, (bottom): Bloomberg; 45: Whataburger; 46: Denver Public Library/Western History Collection; 47: SSPL/Getty Images; 48: Lloyd Hawthorne; 49: Keith Wood; 50–51: Joe McNally/Getty Images; 56: Popperfoto/Getty Images; 57: Michael Ainsworth; 58: The Granger Collection; 59 (left): Kenneth Haftertape/*Southwestern Historical Quarterly*, (right): Dolph Briscoe Center for American History; 60: Jerry Driendl Photography; 61: David Kidd; 66: Richard Michael Pruitt/*Dallas Morning News*; 67 (top left): John Dixon/*The News Gazette*, (buttons at top right): David J. Frent; 68 (left): *Dallas Morning News*, (right): AP Photo/Baylor University Texas Collection via Waco Tribune Herald; 69: Colton, J. H., & Company/UNT Libraries/Portal to Texas History; 70: Hulton Archive/Stringer; 71: Dr. Lawrence D. Lemke/Wayne State University; 72: *Heritage Magazine*/Texas Historical Foundation/Portal to Texas History; 73: Nicholay Stanev; 74: Bettmann/Corbis; 75 (derricks): Time & Life Pictures, (Bass family): AP Photos; 76: UNLV/Special Collections; 77: ssuaphotos; 78 (left): Christian Dumont/REA/Redux, (right): Ron Sachs/CNP/Corbis; 79 (left): Jim Edds/Photo Researchers Inc, (middle): Alexis Rosenfeld/Photo Researchers Inc, (right): Marine Well Containment Company; 80: Reuters/Richard Carson; 81 (top right): Tim Rue/Bloomberg via Getty Images, (bottom): Matthew Staver/Bloomberg via Getty Images; 82: Associated Press; 83: Courtesy of Sam Wyly; 84: Dallas Events Inc.; 85 (left): Jeff Riedel/*Time* Magazine, (right): Nick del la Toree/*Houston Chronicle*; 88: Getty Images; 89: Corbis; 92: Green Mountain Energy; 93 (top): Green Mountain Energy, (bottom): Christian Heeb/laif; 94: Neiman Marcus/*Dallas Morning News*; 95 (left): DeGoyler Library/Southern Methodist University, (right): Neiman Marcus; 96: Smithsonian Institute; 97: Shiner Beers; 98: Roger Ressmeyer/Corbis; 99 (left): Bettman/Corbis, (right): Courtesy of Texas Instruments/Handout/Reuters/Corbis; 104: AP Photo/Rebecca McEntee; 105 (top): AP Photo/Harry Cabluck, (bottom): AP Photo/Harry Cabluck; 106–107: Louie Psihoyos/Science Faction/Corbis; 108: Edward A. Ornelas/*San Antonio Express-News*/Zumapress.com; 109 (clockwise from top): Jay Janner/*Austin American Statesman*, Charlie Vargas, Charlie Vargas; 112: Jill Johnson/*Fort Worth Star-Telegram*/MCT/Getty Images; 113 (top): Jill Johnson/*Fort Worth Star-Telegram*/MCT/Getty Images, (middle): Brent Humphreys/Redux, (bottom): Robyn Beck/AFP/Getty Images; 114 (Mission Church): Bruce Berman, (Cestohowa), Cooke Photo, (Fort Stockton): Mmphotos; 115 (Mo-Ranch): Portal to Texas History, (Risin Sun): Peter Granger/laif/Redux, (Pleasant Grove): Corbis/Ed Darack, (Plano Masjid): Walter Anderson, (Barsana Dham): STR New/Reuters, (Beth Jacob): Nick Saum; 116: Getty Images; 117 (clockwise from top left): Redferns, Southwest Collection/Special Collections Library Texas Tech University, David Redfern/Redferns/Getty Images, AP Photo/*Houston Chronicle*/Dave Einsel, Getty Images; 118: Will van Overbeek; 120: Evans Caglage/*Dallas Morning News*; 121 (top to bottom): Courtesy Half-Price Books, Courtesy Half-Price Books, Richard Michael; 122: Bruce Dale/National Geographic Stock; 124: Chinati Foundation; 125 (clockwise from top left): Getty Images, Barclay Gibson, Warner Bros/Photofest, Associated Press; 126: Sean Meyers/Gallery Stock; 127 (clockwise from top left): Jim Sugar/Corbis, Rolf Nussbaumer Photography, Jim Parkin/Shutterstock, James Barker and Co./University of Texas at Arlington Library/Portal to Texas History; 128: Phillip Lange; 129 (clockwise from top left): JupiterImages, Bo Zaunders/Corbis, Klaus Nigge/National Geographic Stock, Larry Lee Photography, Andy Mahr/Gallery Stock; 132: The History Center/Diboll, Texas; 133: Texas Forest Service; 134: Cushing Memorial Library and Archives/Texas A&M University; 135 (top): Cushing Memorial Library and Archives/Texas A&M University, (bottom): CIMMYT; 137: Dan Winters; 138: Library of Congress; 139 (clockwise from top left): Jonathan Sprague/Redux, Andrew Baranowski/Getty Images, Gordon Gahan/National Geographic/Getty Images, Library of Congress; 146-147: Gary Irving/Panoramic Images; 148: David Woo/*Dallas Morning News*; 149 (clockwise from top left): Hulton Archive, *Dallas Morning News*, Phil Huber/*Dallas Morning News*, Getty Images; 150: AP Photo; 151 (top): Wikipedia Public Domain, (middle): Gregg Mack; 152 (top): NFL Historical Imagery, (inset): Andrew D. Bernstein/Getty Images; 153: Wally McNamee/Corbis; 154–155: Laura Wilson; 156: Michael Ochs Archives/Getty Images; 157: Lisa Eisner; 158: Rafiq Maqbool/Corbis; 159 (clockwise from top right): George H. W. Bush Library, Erich Schlegel, AP Photo; 160: Bettmann/Corbis/AP Images; 161 (left): Richard Michael Pruitt/*Dallas Morning News*, (right): Andy Scott/*Dallas Morning News*; 162: AP Photo/Lauren Victoria Burke; 163 (clockwise from top): AP Photo/Doug Mills, AP Photo/Ricardo Thomas, AP Photo/*Detroit News*/ Ricardo Thomas; 166: AP Photo/Itsuo Inouye; 167: Courtesy of the Federal Reserve Bank of Dallas and Richard Fisher/Information sourced from the Bureau of Labor Statistics and the Federal Reserve Bank of Dallas; Back flap: Karen Sanders; Back cover (clockwise from top left): Joe McNally/Getty Images, Gillespie County Historical Society, Erich Schlegel, Getty Images, AP Photo, VisionsofAmerica/Joe Sohn, SSPL/Getty Images, Paul Gaither, Will van Overbeek, Time & Life Pictures

INFOGRAPHIC SOURCES:

14: Unviersal Map Group LLC; 19: Archives.gov, nytimes.com; 24–25: Texas General Land Office; 40–41: National Conference of State Legislators, The Texas State Senate, The Texas House of Representatives, Ballotpedia.org, Texastribune.org; 42–43: *Automotive News*, Center for Automotive Research, Congressional Research Service, Kentucky Cabinet for Economic Development, Economic Development Partnership of Alabama, Office of Aerospace and Automotive Industry/U.S. Department of Commerce; 52–53: Census.gov, Bureau of Transportation Statistics, Federal Highway Administration, Bexar County Economic Development; 54–55: Waterborne Commerce Statistics Center, US Army Corps of Engineers, Navigation Data Center, Statistics and Models Administration Unit/Panama Canal, Texas Ports Association; 62–63: U.S. Census Bureau, Jon Bruner/Forbes.com, "The Texas Economy"/Texas Comptroller of Public Accounts; 64–65: U.S. Bureau of Labor Statistics, U.S. Census Bureau, Texas Office of the Governor, Moody's North American Business Cost Review, Dallas Regional Chamber *Economic Development Guide*; 78–79: American Petroleum Institute, The National Ocean Industries Association, National Academy of Engineering, BP Commission, Billy Pugh Company, American Oil & Gas Historical Society, Red Adair Company, The National Academies, Marine Technology Society, U.S. Geological Survey, Oceaneering International, Offshore Technology Conference, U.S. Energy Information Administration, Shell; 86–87: U.S. Energy Information Administration; 90–91: Electric Reliability Council of Texas, Wind Technologies Market Report, Lawrence Berkeley National Laboratory, Texas Commission on Environmental Quality; 100–101: *Fortune* 500, Renaissance Capital; 102–103: *Chief Executive* magazine, Waste Management, *The Orange County Register*, Houston Chronicle, Costar.com, *Dayton Daily News*, *The Austin-American Statesman*, *Pegasus News*, CCS Medical, *The New York Times*, Greyhound, *The Chicago Tribune*, KCRA, Kimberly-Clark, Fluor EPCM Services, Hanger Orthopedic Group, Telmar Network Technology, *The Dallas Morning News*; 110–111: Bureau of Labor Statistics; 130–131: Economic Research Service/USDA, National Agricultural Statistics Service/USDA; 140–141: 2012 Small Business Survey/Thumbtack.com, State of California/Franchise Tax Board, Texas Comptroller of Public Accounts, Little Hoover Commission/State of California; 142–143: Cost of Living Index/The Council for Community and Economic Research, Fuel Gauge Report/AAA; 144–145: Real Estate Market Report/Zillow Local Info, City of Chicago, International City/County Management Association, *The Wall Street Journal*, Center for Housing Policy/Housing Landscape 2012; 164–165: Texas Medical Board, Texas Medical Association, Texas Wide Open for Business, Texans for Lawsuit Reform, Harris County District Clerk, Texas Medical Liability Trust

ACKNOWLEDGMENTS

We would like to thank Bob Dolan, dean of the Business School at the University of Michigan, whose thought provoking question, "How can Michigan become more like Texas?" was the inspiration for this book.

It's the same issue that Dallas Fed Chief Richard Fisher, one of our Texas Game-Changers, and John Engler, the former governor of Michigan, addressed during the July 2012 "Jobs for America" panel at the Milken Institute's Global Conference in Los Angeles. Engler opened the panel by stating that Michigan (his home state) and California (his host state)—indeed, the whole country—need to become more like Texas. Fisher went even further, "re-writing" George Strait's famous song, "All My Exes Live in Texas": "It's not just ex-wives, but ex-businesses, ex-employers, ex-taxpayers and ex-voters of Michigan and California (and New York and other areas of the country) who are pulling up stakes and coming to live a new life and thrive in Texas."

We hope *Texas Got It Right!* provides an entertaining, educational, and inspiring road map to help get the rest of our great country on the path to success that Texas continues to chart.

We would also like to thank the following people for their significant contributions to this book:

Walter Isaacson, a friend and fellow Louisianan and the distinguished biographer of *Steve Jobs*, *Einstein: His Life and Universe*, *Benjamin Franklin: An American Life*, and *Kissinger: A Biography*, for infusing the foreword with his southern charm, clever wit, and unique historical, cultural, and economic perspective.

Laura Wilson, acclaimed photographer and mother of filmmakers Andrew, Owen and Luke, for allowing us to use a few of her extraordinary photos from her quintessentially Texas book, *Grit and Glory: Six-Man Football*.

Karen Sanders, a migrant to Texas by way of Tennessee, California, Arizona, and Illinois, for her keen interest in and understanding of history, and for always being there with the right words, ideas, and images.

Susan Tiholiz, a Kentuckian by birth who has come to love Texas even more while working on this project, for her insight and intelligence, and for always trying her best to keep us on time and on track.

Karen Wade, for getting things done—even when everyone else says it's impossible. Her smile, kind heart, and relentless determination are invaluable assets.

Charlie Vargas, Andrew's close friend and a very talented photographer from Dallas, for his images of Austin and the SXSW Festival.

David McAninch, who joined the project at just the right time, for his quick intellect and acute editing skills. He was a pleasure to work with, and his contributions improved the book in many ways.

The team at Melcher Media, Lauren Nathan, Gabriella Paiella, and Duncan Bock, for their many creative and editorial contributions.

Evan Wyly and Mitchell Wyly, for their edits on the "10 Ways to Become More Like Texas" page.

Sam's Aggie wife, Cheryl, and all our family, for the happiness and joy that their support and love bring to us each and every day.

Melcher Media would like to thank Chika Azuma, Kay Banning, Chris Beha, Adam Bright, David E. Brown, Holly Dolce, Shannon Fanuko, Melissa Goldstein, David McAninch, Myles McDonnell, Naomi Mizusaki, Cheryl Della Pietra, Julia Sourikoff, Michel Vrana, and Megan Worman.

Produced by

MELCHER MEDIA
124 West 13th Street
New York, NY 10011
www.melcher.com

Publisher: Charles Melcher
Associate Publisher: Bonnie Eldon
Editor in Chief: Duncan Bock
Editor and Project Manager: Lauren Nathan
Text Editor: David McAninch
Infographic Researcher: Adam Bright
Production Director: Kurt Andrews
Editorial Intern: Gabriella Paiella

Designed by Naomi Mizusaki, Supermarket
Additional design work by Chika Azuma
Cover design by Michel Vrana
Photo research by Melissa Goldstein